1. Every person:
    Wants to feel valued
                          Respected
2.
3.   appreciated
4.   Understood

FROM PAYCHECK TO
PURPOSE

I press on toward the goal to win the prize
for which God has called me heavenward in Christ Jesus.
—Philippians 3:14 NIV

FROM PAYCHECK TO
PURPOSE

The Clear Path
to Doing Work
You Love

KEN COLEMAN

RAMSEY
P R E S S

Published by Ramsey Press, The Lampo Group, LLC
Franklin, Tennessee 37064

Dave Ramsey, *The Ramsey Show*, EveryDollar, Financial Peace, *Financial Peace University*, *The Legacy Journey, Smart Money Smart Kids*, Rachel Cruze, *The Total Money Makeover*, *Retire Inspired*, and *Business Boutique* are all registered trademarks of Lampo Licensing, LLC. All rights reserved.

This publication is designed to provide accurate and authoritative information with regard to the subject matter covered. It is sold with the understanding that the publisher is not engaged in rendering financial, accounting, or other professional advice. If financial advice or other expert assistance is required, the services of a competent professional should be sought.

Scripture quotations marked CEV are from the Contemporary English Version Copyright © 1991, 1992, 1995 by American Bible Society, Used by Permission.

Scripture quotations marked ESV are from the ESV® Bible (The Holy Bible, English Standard Version®). ESV® Text Edition: 2016. Copyright © 2001 by Crossway, a publishing ministry of Good News Publishers. The ESV® text has been reproduced in cooperation with and by permission of Good News Publishers. Unauthorized reproduction of this publication is prohibited. All rights reserved.

Scripture quotations marked NIV are from the Holy Bible, New International Version®, NIV®. Copyright © 1973, 1978, 1984, 2011 by Biblica, Inc.™ Used by permission of Zondervan. All rights reserved worldwide. www.zondervan.com. The "NIV" and "New International Version" are trademarks registered in the United States Patent and Trademark Office by Biblica, Inc.™

The names and other identifying facts of individuals whose stories appear in this book have been changed to protect their privacy.

Editors: Jennifer Day and Rachel Knapp
Cover Design: Chris Carrico and Gretchen Hyer
Photography: Seth Farmer
Interior Design: PerfecType, Nashville, TN

ISBN: 978-1-942121-53-4

Library of Congress Cataloging-in-Publication Data

Names: Coleman, Ken (Radio talk show host) author.
Title: From paycheck to purpose: the clear path to doing work you love / Ken
    Coleman.
Identifiers: LCCN 2021029158 | ISBN 9781942121534 (hardback)
Subjects: LCSH: Self-actualization (Psychology) | Motivation (Psychology) |
    Success.
Classification: LCC BF637.S4 C65225 2021 | DDC 158.1--dc23
LC record available at https://lccn.loc.gov/2021029158

Printed in the United States of America
21 22 23 24 WRZ 5 4 3 2 1

CONTENTS

Foreword by Dave Ramsey   vii

Acknowledgments   xi

Introduction   1

Stage 1: Get Clear on What You Were Born to Do

Chapter 1   Clarity Is Your Superpower   11

Chapter 2   The Simple Way to Get Clear   23

Stage 2: Get Qualified for the Work You Want to Do

Chapter 3   The Four Questions to Get You in the Door   43

Chapter 4   The Secret to Sticking with It   61

Stage 3: Get Connected for Opportunities

Chapter 5   You Already Know Everyone You Need to Know   79

Chapter 6   The Art of Connecting   95

Stage 4: Get Started on the Journey

Chapter 7   The Enemies of Progress   119

Chapter 8   Start the Right Way   139

Stage 5: Get Promoted up the Ladder

Chapter 9   Win the Now to Get to the Next   161

Chapter 10 Five Qualities That Bring Promotions to You   177

Stage 6: Get Your Dream Job

Chapter 11 How to Tell the Difference Between the Dream
               and a Mirage   199

Chapter 12 How to Keep the Dream from Becoming
               a Nightmare   219

Stage 7: Give Yourself Away to Work Like No One Else

Chapter 13 Expand Your Vision   239

Conclusion   249

Notes   253

FOREWORD
BY DAVE RAMSEY

For thirty years, fifteen hours a week, I've been taking calls on a national talk radio show from people with money questions. And I've found there are really only two sides to the money equation: the income side and the outgo side. Most of the questions I get are about the outgo side. People want to know what to do with money once they've gotten it. They want to know how to get out of debt, build wealth, and make wise decisions with their hard-earned cash. But oftentimes when I dig into the backstory and the life of the caller, I find that they are really facing an income problem . . . which usually reveals they're struggling with career issues or even worse—a career crisis.

Career-building and finding work that matters in America today is about as American as apple pie. But the reality is, the quest for a dream job plays out in tandem with all of the sidetracks, setbacks, and stupid decisions of real life. Along the way, people realize that pursuing a slice of the pie doesn't always guarantee that they'll actually *love* what they do and why they do it. Instead of growing their greatest wealth-building tool—their income—they find themselves trapped living paycheck to paycheck, which causes a divide between their approach to money and meaningful work. They begin to believe that money and meaning can't coexist. In fact, people often fear they have to take a dumbed-down income in order to find work that has meaning. So, they stay stuck in a soul-sucking J-O-B, believing the lie that you can't have your dream career *and* the income to go with it. But money and meaning can and should exist together, if done right. And Ken Coleman will show you how.

Ken has the experience and has done the research to silence your fears, answer your questions, and help you get out of a career crisis or avoid one altogether. My first pastor used to say, "A man with an experience is not at the mercy of a man with an opinion." Ken and I have been friends for several decades, and I can tell you he's been in the trenches. The information he offers in this book comes not just from theoretical constructs, it also comes from his personal journey and the journeys of the thousands of people he's successfully coached. People who hated their current jobs and saw no way out. People who didn't know the first thing about writing a resumé, growing their skills, making professional connections, or getting promoted. People who were too busy paying bills to dream about their true purpose. Ken has seen it all and has developed a clear and practical path that comes from real-world know-how.

Like a lot of books that come from Ramsey Solutions, this one puts the responsibility on you to implement its principles. Let's face it, we can give you all the plans in the world, but if you don't put them into action, then you won't experience the change you're wanting in your life. You are the variable that has the most impact on your future.

You've got to get up, leave the cave, kill something, and drag it home. You have to *get with it*.

There are a lot of *gets* in this book. As a matter of fact, Ken lays out a plan with six things you have to *get* and one that you have to *give* to be successful. The very words *get* and *give* indicate that this process is on you. If you will follow this very clear path, it will work. It will not work without bumps in the road. It will not work without fog and rain. It will not work without disappointment. But if you persist and follow this path, it will work every time.

I'm so proud of the journey that Ken is going to lead you on. And I'm so proud of where you're going to end up as a result of this book. It will cause you to not just *get* the career you've always dreamed about but also *get* the life that God intended for you.

Now, *get after it!*

ACKNOWLEDGMENTS

A finished book is a testament to the team that took an idea and made it a reality. I am so blessed to be a part of a team of All-Stars!

I must first thank my home team, Stacy, Ty, Chase, and Josie. Stacy, your unfailing love and never-ending encouragement give me strength. To our kids, your curiosity and support lift me.

Dave Ramsey, thank you for believing in this message, for giving me this opportunity, and for modeling the clear path.

Preston Cannon, you are a master of the publishing process, and your leadership makes a daunting task doable.

Kris Bearss, what a joy it was to work with you. Your prodding, patience, and prose made this book a reality, and your passion for the message inspired me.

Jennifer Day, no one uses a smile and a suggestion better than you do. Your guidance is brilliant. You are simply the best.

Damon Goude, thank you for your steady and strong hand in how you lead, support, and equip me to do the work I'm called to do.

Chris Carrico, Gretchen Hyer, and Seth Farmer, thanks for the creative direction and brilliant design of the book cover.

Rachel Knapp, thank you for your meticulous and invaluable copyediting.

Amy McCollom, thanks for handling the myriad of details to keep the train on the tracks and on schedule.

Caitlin Cofield, Jeff Miller, Megan McConnell, Will Case, and Mckenzie Masters, thank you for your superpowers of promotion through world-class marketing and publicity.

Jeremy Breland, Suzanne Simms, and Jen Sievertsen, thank you for your leadership, input, and support throughout the process.

INTRODUCTION

I have no idea what to do! I'm desperate and I need help!"

Allison's voice shook as she spoke.

"I've been in the same job for twelve years. The owner recently sold the company, and I can see the writing on the wall: my days are numbered. I've been applying for jobs, trying to find something before I get laid off."

"How has that gone?" I asked.

"That's why I'm scared," she admitted, choking back tears. "It's been three months of constant applications and changing my resumé, and I've had what I felt were really good interviews. But not one offer. Every time I get an interview, my hopes go up—and then they're shattered just as quickly when I hear they've hired someone else."

The words just kept pouring out, revealing a jumble of thoughts and emotions.

"We can't make it without my salary. It's so serious that my husband and I have discussed selling our house and moving in with my parents. But that's a worst-case scenario because living with them would be really hard on our relationship. I just fell into my current job and am so confused about what I want to do, but I feel like I can't even think about that right now. At the moment, I need any job I can get. I'll work fast food, retail—whatever I need to. But how we'll replace my benefits and salary in another line of work . . . I don't have a clue."

Allison sounded hopeless. "It tears me apart to put my family in a situation like this. I have no idea how we'll break this to the kids if I can't find something soon."

Allison isn't alone in her struggle.

Too Good to Be True?

The fact that you've opened this book tells me you're looking to grow your career to an entirely new level. You might be looking for your next job. You could be miserable in your current one. Or maybe you're a seasoned professional who knows there's more, but you're not sure what to do or how to get there.

You may be feeling . . .

Stuck in your current job, doing the same thing year after year.

Scared to death of losing your job and at a loss about what direction to take.

Discouraged by all those job applications that you've never heard back from.

Overwhelmed and paralyzed at the thought of switching careers.

So bored that you're watching your soul dry up just a little more each year.

Or maybe, for as long as you can remember, the possibility of getting to do something you love has always seemed like a lost cause. So you've just been getting by . . .

Sucking it up in a job you can't stand.

Demoralized every day by office politics, shoddy leadership, or a toxic culture.

Burned out by your boss's crazy demands and unrealistic deadlines.

Doubting your career choice and even your purpose for living.

This book will help you with all of those things. But we have to start by addressing a much bigger question that we all face: Is there even such a thing as a dream job, and is it too much to hope that it can happen for you?

Most people think dream jobs are about as real as unicorns and that only a tiny percentage of people are lucky enough to find one. A "good" job—work that you can tolerate with decent pay and benefits—is as good as it gets.

A dream job where you get paid for doing work you love? That sounds too good to be true. *Insanely unrealistic* may be a better way to say it. If you're like just about everyone else on the planet, your experience is that *nobody* gets the job they want. That only happens to celebrities, child prodigies, and maybe the valedictorian from your senior class. Your grandparents didn't ever have a job they loved. Your parents didn't. Your friends don't. And you sure don't.

In your world—*the real world*—there's no time for dreams or dream jobs. The bills, the family, all of the responsibilities of life won't wait. . . .

Hold on.

I know why you're thinking that.

I once thought the same things.

I was the guy with no degree, miserable in my day job but riddled with doubt about making a change. My head told me I was *way* too old to start over in a career I *might* like. I had a family to feed for crying out loud! There was no time to even think about a dream job, let alone pursue one.

But that's exactly what I ended up doing. And I'm here to tell you that not only do dream jobs exist, but they exist for everyday, ordinary people like you and me.

Have you ever stopped to wonder how it is that the thought of having a job you love never completely leaves you? You can try to silence it, rationalize it, ignore it, but it's always there, asking, "What if?"

There's a reason for that. There's a reason you can't shake the feeling that there's something more you're meant to do. And it has to do with why you were put on this earth. As I talk to people from all walks of life on my show, they have one thing in common. No matter how hopeless, defeated, or confused they feel, they always come back to one thing—they want to make a difference in the world.

Every single one of us carries that desire with us until the day we die. It's built in. And one of the most meaningful ways to make a difference is through work that matters. Doing work that lights up your soul is life-changing—for you and for everyone around you. So even if I haven't met you yet, I know that much about you already. Despite your doubts, you want to believe your dream job is out there. You hope it's real. And you'd like to stop thinking about it and start living it for yourself.

A Clear Path

Some of you are very skeptical that finding and doing your dream job is possible. All I ask is that you trust my belief in you and give me the privilege of your time over the next thirteen chapters—with your heart and mind wide open and all in.

I begin every broadcast of *The Ken Coleman Show* by saying, "You were created to fill a unique role. You are needed. You must do it." And I mean it. You have something extraordinary to give—but that also means you have an obligation to figure out what role that is and then actually do it. Why? *Because somebody out there needs you to be you!*

What most people never discover is that there's a very clear path to your dream job. And by the time you're done reading this book, you'll be equipped with a practical process—seven sequential stages—for discovering and doing the work you were meant to do. You're going to learn how to:

1. **Get Clear** on the work you were uniquely made to do and why.
2. **Get Qualified** to do the work you were created for.
3. **Get Connected** with the right people who can open the doors to your dream.
4. **Get Started** by overcoming the emotions and mistakes that often hold people back.

5. (Get Promoted) by developing winning habits and traits.
6. (Get Your Dream Job) to do work you love and produce results that matter to you.
7. (Give Yourself Away) by expanding the dream to leave a legacy.

The stages are simple, but the journey is not.

On this journey, you'll begin to approach your job search differently. You'll learn to ask different questions. You'll look at work differently. Instead of working to live, you'll be *living* to work, to create, to contribute as only you can. You'll probably get knocked down—but you'll keep getting back up.

That's the difference between those who reach their dream job and those who don't. To live the dream, you have to listen to your heart. Let's make sure nothing gets in the way of that.

"But, Ken, I don't have a clue what kind of work I would love."

"I didn't get the right degree."

"I've waited too long."

"I have no network."

"I'll never get the interview."

"I'm scared to try something different."

"My bosses don't even know I exist."

"I'm feeling beat down and demotivated."

"What if I fail?"

I get it. I've said what you're saying and have felt what you're feeling. I remember how suffocating the fog of a J-O-B is. Your work is draining you, but you can't see past the fears, doubts, and uncertainties to try something different. Here's the good news, though: If you can't stand your job right now, it's not a life sentence. You can change your situation!

I've tested the process within these pages in my own life, doing every single thing I suggest to you. It worked for me, and it's worked for the people who listen to the show and use our resources.

So all the stuff you've read in other books or online? Set it aside for now. Let's get a fresh start by taking a different approach than everybody else.

Most of the world spends their life in a job they hate—but they won't do anything to change it. I have one response to that: *You can be a little uncomfortable for a while, or you can be terribly miserable every Monday for the rest of your life.*

By reading this book, you're signaling that you've decided to do something about this now, as opposed to spending ten more years watching your soul leave your body at the start of every workweek. Dig out the dream you've stuffed away in the attic, dust it off, and let it see the light of day. Give it—and yourself—another chance.

This is your moment.

You were born with a purpose. You were created to fulfill a unique role. You are needed. You have work to do that matters.

Let's look at how to exit the daily grind, get to the heart of your *why*, and start living your dream once and for all.

This works if you work. I'll give you my all, but I'm also asking you to give me yours.

You already have what it takes. You really, really do. And it starts right now.

Get Clear on What You Were Born to Do

1

Clarity Is Your Superpower

It was two o'clock in the morning and our house was completely quiet—the kids tucked in their beds, my wife sleeping peacefully next to me.

Me? I was restless, miserable, and exhausted, unable to sleep because I was the main character in my own horror movie, *Sleepless in Suckville*.

This had been going on for months. Sleep should have been automatic. Stacy and I—with three kids under the age of three—were in that intense season of parenting where just sitting down for thirty seconds can put you in a coma.

Instead, I was watching my bedside clock count down the hours—a visual of the clock of my life—and all I could think was, *I'm five years away from forty. My career is going nowhere. I've wasted so much of my life!*

Watching infomercials was my only escape from the agony I felt. They not only distracted me, they also made me feel a little better: things could be worse—I could be one of THOSE guys! Deep down, though, I kind of envied those people. They at least looked like they were doing something they loved.

On the surface, I had nothing to complain about. On paper, our life in the Atlanta suburbs was everything you could ask for. The little business I owned was doing okay. My wife and I liked our neighborhood, and everyone was healthy. There was food on our table and we were grateful. So why was I so down? Why couldn't I sleep?

Because I knew I wasn't doing what I was born to do. It didn't matter that everything looked good from the outside. My J-O-B was sucking the life out of me. It was extremely hard to get started every day but super easy to get distracted. I was selling something I didn't care about and had no desire to keep doing it. I knew there was more, but I felt stuck.

For an optimistic, energetic guy like me, this was a bitter pill to swallow. Day after day after day, I felt like I was running on a treadmill with no way to stop and nowhere to go even if I could.

To make matters worse, I was also grieving. I'd recently realized that the career I'd prepared for my entire adult life—the work everybody said I was born for—wasn't my dream job after all. I'd worked two congressional campaigns, served on a governor's staff . . . and was supposed to be running for public office by now. Instead, I'd lost my passion. I didn't feel I could make a difference in a system I'd lost faith in. The *politics* of politics had killed my vision for a long career in public service.

Staring at this dead end shook me. I had thought politics was *it*. But my dream had died and taken my hope with it. And as I stared at the TV screen, I only had one thought: *I really don't need those knives. What I need is a new direction.*

Plagued by Doubt

The one good thing about this mess was that my restlessness constantly nudged me to keep searching for meaningful work. While driving to a meeting or watching one of those infomercials, I'd toss around different career scenarios. Being an ideas guy, I could easily visualize a dozen paths to take—some of which seemed pretty exciting, including broadcasting.

In the moments where I'd let myself dream a little, I'd remember that for my whole life, whenever I'd done anything in front of an audience, I would get the juice, loving every minute of it. And I thought I had the raw talent.

Sometimes I'd actually visualize myself in a studio, asking influential people questions about interesting topics . . . but almost immediately the inner dialogue would start: *Uh, Ken, reality check! No one in broadcasting knows who you are. You have zero experience and no degree. And you're too old to break into the industry. Wake up, dude, this dream ain't happening! You should just go do your job and save yourself a lot of disappointment.*

As I began to believe the voice of doubt, the painful regrets would kick in: *I have wasted so much of my life! If only I'd chosen a better career in the first place. I should have pursued broadcasting when my whole life was ahead of me. There's no way I'll ever have a show of my own at this point. . . .*

It was like my heart and my head were in a constant argument. One moment I would be excited about the possibilities—the next moment, sick with the thought I might be delusional. It was like riding a roller coaster, up and down, curve after curve, loop after loop. I knew

I couldn't keep doing this much longer. My heart couldn't handle it. I needed some direction.

Decision Point

That season of disappointment and confusion wasn't just a professional problem; it was a personal one. Looking back, I can see that my crisis was created by a lack of clarity. I wasn't clear on what direction to take, what particular work fit me best, or even how to get to my dream job if I *did* figure it out. I was more confused than a chameleon in a bowl of Skittles.

Have you been there? That painful intersection between "Not Happy" and "Don't Know What to Do About It"? Are you there now—afraid it's too late? Worried that even if you get a break, you don't have the talent? If so, you're not alone!

A 2019 online survey (prepandemic) revealed that almost 65 percent of employees were thinking of leaving their jobs in 2020.[1] According to US government labor statistics, the average American adult doesn't just change jobs once or twice between ages twenty-five and fifty-two but *six times or more!*[2] Other research says that almost 50 percent of all the workers surveyed have changed *careers*, not just jobs, at least once. The main reason? They were unhappy.[3] American employees feel so disappointed in their work that nine out of ten told the *Harvard Business Review* they would take a pay cut if it meant doing more meaningful work.[4] In other words, meaning matters more than money! But the good news is, this book will show you how to get meaning *and* money from your work. Stay tuned.

I've shared some of the misery in my story because I want you to know *I get it*. All of it. The reason I do what I do—the reason *The Ken Coleman Show* exists—is because I have lived in this purgatory of personal and professional misery. I won't ever forget feeling like I didn't have anything to offer, doubting I would ever make a difference, fearing that if I found my path I wouldn't be able to complete it. And now it's one of the greatest joys of my life to help others overcome those feelings, get unstuck, and move forward to make their unique contribution and achieve their dreams.

So where does this massive, life-altering journey begin? With clarity.

Clarity Is Your Key

"What should I do with my life?"

"My current job has great benefits. Should I stay put even though I don't love it?"

"I've always wanted to try something different, but is it just too unrealistic?"

The path to meaningful work starts by getting clear because *clarity is the key to unlocking your future.*

What is clarity? It's "the quality of being certain or definite" or something that is "easy to see or hear."[5] For our journey together, *clarity* means

- being certain of WHO you are,
- WHAT contribution you want to make, and
- WHY you want to make that impact.

When you're clear on who you are, the contribution you make in the workplace, and why the impact of your contribution matters to you, you have the ability to navigate any uncertainty that confronts you on your path.

What does that mean for you? *A lot.*

Getting clear helps you *identify* your dream job.

It gives you the *confidence* to step out on the path.

And it gives you the *courage* to stay on that path no matter how rough it gets.

Most of the people I talk with on the show are locked up about their work in some way. They don't have clarity. So while I ask practical questions, I'm especially listening for what makes that person's pulse quicken (for all the good reasons) as we talk. This tells me things their resumé never could. In the short time we have together, my goal is to hear and read each caller's heart back to them so they can realize their own answer.

I will never be the expert on them—but *they* are! Deep inside of them are the answers about what they were made to do and why. My job is to help pick the lock.

I remember one caller to the show named Michelle. She had given up her career path a decade earlier to raise her daughter but was now back in the workforce. After listening to the show for a while, Michelle realized she'd only been hopping from one dead-end job to another just to make ends meet. There was no purpose or passion in her work—and she wanted more.

She sat down at her kitchen table one night and started getting clear. She knew she enjoyed working in health insurance, helping people get the medicine they needed at a specialty pharmacy. She researched careers within specialty pharmacy and found a position that traveled to doctors' offices helping doctors and patients get access to specialty medications. I gave her some suggestions, and she revised her resumé and applied for the position. Within just a few weeks, she was offered the job and went from making $30,000 a year to $100,000! Michelle's story is not a miracle—it's predictable. Her story illustrates the super-power of clarity.

With clarity, you can experience your own breakthrough. *You* are the expert on you. *You* are capable of changing your destiny. And you already have the answers you need. I'm just going to help you get unlocked so you can see them.

The Impact of Clarity

In baseball, when a batter hits the ball in just the right place—the sweet spot—he or she can barely feel the contact with the ball, but everyone can see the result. I don't know how to say it except that it just . . . looks and feels right. Almost effortless. The contact is perfect—the ball liter-ally jumps off the bat and travels farther and faster.

What does clarity do for you? It lets you *see* the ball and keep your eyes on it so you can perform to your potential and create maximum impact. It helps you hit meaningful home runs in your work, day after day.

As soon as you experience work in your sweet spot, you'll know it! The maximum impact this creates will feel natural to you. Your head will know it and your heart will feel it.

Now it makes sense why successful athletes are so confident, right? They've found the sweet spot. Having clarity works the same way for us. Being clear frees us to look at job opportunities and say, "If the job involves this, I know I can do it well. And I'll love it. And it will make my heart full."

Thirty years of research backs me up on this. If you've ever experienced one of those practically effortless situations, you were experiencing a mental state psychologists refer to as *flow*.

The leading researcher in this field is a guy with a name that just rolls off the tongue: Mihaly Csikszentmihalyi (pronounced *Me-high CHICK-sent-me-high-ee*). Mihaly is a professor of psychology at Claremont Graduate University and the originator of flow theory. He compares flow to playing jazz: "Your whole being is involved, and you're using your skills to the utmost."[6]

His description of flow sounds a lot like working in your sweet spot: You're in the flow when your "sense of time disappears, you forget yourself, you feel part of something larger. . . . What you are doing becomes worth doing for its own sake. . . . You are doing what you really like to do."[7] When you're in the flow, the work is energizing and the results are extraordinary.

When I think about people I've admired who found their sweet spot, one of the first names that pops into my mind is Benny Polk, my spitfire basketball coach from high school. Coach Polk was such a natural that he even looked cool in those dreadful short shorts that coaches wore back in the day! I always picture him with a whistle around his neck and an intense look on his face.

He loved practice as much as he loved games, and he had a way of teaching the X's and O's so anyone could get it. A good practice made him as happy as a win. You've never seen a guy so excited for his players to execute a drill, master a fundamental, excel in the classroom—or win in life. Coach made teaching a bunch of teenagers look easy. All day, every day. His skill, enthusiasm, and values came together powerfully—and his impact on me and many others was huge.

Finding Your Flow

How do you get to your sweet spot, like Coach Polk, and find that flow? By getting clear about the three primary gifts we're all given:

1. Your **talent**—what you do best
2. Your **passion**—the work you love to do most
3. Your **mission**—the results of your work that matter deeply to you

When you're operating from this place, there's nothing like it. What a lot of people miss, though, is that to find your sweet spot you need to be clear on *all* three gifts.

Using only your *talent* can make you successful.

Using your *talent* to perform your *passion* can give you some job satisfaction. *Success To Significance*

But using your *talent* to perform your *passion* to fulfill your *mission*? That's when you find significance. And the success and satisfaction you long for come with achieving significance in your work.

There was a time when I thought sports radio might be *the* area of broadcasting for me. Once I got a taste of that world through some small gigs, though, I realized my love for sports didn't translate into a love for *talking* sports for three hours every day. After a while, I started to feel empty. Sports radio didn't fulfill that third part of me: the results I wanted most.

As I considered that piece of the puzzle, I got clear on my purpose, which was to *use my public communication skills to help people maximize their potential.* Had I stuck with sports radio, I would have just been performing to entertain. But my mission—the results I desired most— kept me on the path to discovering my purpose.

The way Courtney, a caller on my show, described the feeling is as good a description as any I've heard. She said, "Ken, I'm struggling with getting clear on the mission part. I can't come up with anything." After she told me what her results would be under *talent*, she moved on to *passion* and mentioned how she loved connecting people to useful health-and-wellness resources.

"Why health and wellness?" I asked. "Be specific."

"Because I had a breakthrough in my life," she said, "a total physical transformation." BINGO! Courtney had just revealed the result of her work that she cared deeply about and the reason it mattered so much. She wanted to help other people experience physical transformation. I remember smiling big, knowing her light bulb had just switched on. All that was left was to ask her a question to get her heart to feel what her brain had just realized. So I said, "What if you could do that all day, every day, knowing you helped somebody transform their life the way you transformed your own?"

"Ken, it would be unspeakable," Courtney replied.

That's it! That's the whole point of what we're doing in these two chapters. When talent, passion and mission come together in your sweet spot, your heart sings, and you feel the juice!

Clarity is so critical, folks! No other chapter in this book will make sense without it.

Want to know what to do with your life? Want to find your dream job and go after it? I can absolutely tell you that the answer comes down to this: get clear on who you are!

You've got to get clear, and then you've got to go after it. This is your time. We'll talk about *how* to do that next.

C'mon, turn the page. I can't wait!

Chapter 1 Takeaways

Remember This

You were created to fill a unique role in this world.

You Got This

You are incredibly valuable!

Do This

Commit to the process of self-discovery in this book.

2

The Simple Way to Get Clear

On April 26, 1967, Dr. Martin Luther King Jr. stood up to speak in a high school auditorium in Cleveland, Ohio. Seated in front of him were rows of mostly black students. Many were scarred by the painful years of racism and violence they had endured and were still enduring.

What did he talk about?

What's the one thing he wanted those young people to know?

That their lives counted.

That the world needed them.

Dr. King told these young people to "develop within [y]ourselves a deep sense of somebodiness. Don't let anybody make you feel that you are nobody. . . . Set out to do a good job, and do that job so well that nobody can do it any better.

If it falls your lot to be a street sweeper, sweep streets like Michelangelo painted pictures.

"Sweep streets like Shakespeare wrote poetry.

"Sweep streets like Beethoven composed music.

"Sweep streets so well that all the hosts of heaven and earth will have to pause and say here lived a great street sweeper who swept his job well."[8]

I imagine that Dr. King would say the same to each one of us today. You matter, and the work you do matters. You are not a nobody. *You* are somebody. And in your work and your life, someone somewhere needs you to show up every day with a deep sense of somebodiness and be the best version of you.

Get Clear, Stage 1 on the path to meaningful work, makes that possible.

If you've tried to do something like this before and it didn't work, stay with me. If you'll follow the steps in this section, you *will* get clear. And it probably won't take as long as you expect.

How to Get Clear

With the five exercises below, you'll discover your must-haves for your dream job. You'll be writing a personalized job description of sorts—but way better. It will feature your best abilities and qualities, the tasks you love to do, and the results from your work that fire up your soul! Your talent, your passion, your mission, and your sweet spot will all be present and accounted for, revealing your professional purpose, your *why* at work, and building your foundation for every stage ahead. By the end of this chapter, you won't just be clear on what work makes you come alive. You'll be amazed at how the path to your dream job has started to open up.

Let's look at the five essential actions that you must take to clarify who you are and what work you were created to do.

Action 1: Get Clear on Your Unique Gifts

Action 1 will help you discover your unique gifts, and you'll refer to them again and again on your journey:

1. Your **talent**—what you do best
2. Your **passion**—the work you love to do most
3. Your **mission**—the results from your work that matter deeply to you

Let's assume your career has a dashboard, and talent, passion, and mission are the gauges you need to keep an eye on. Going forward we'll call these your "Gift Indicators." Like the speedometer, temperature, and fuel indicators in your car, you always want these "readings" to be in the correct range for maximum performance. Being able to trust that your talent, passion, and mission are all engaged and functioning together is what keeps you driving toward your dream job.

As you begin this exercise, grab a notepad and a pencil, and find a quiet place. Now I know some of you are thinking, *A pencil? Ken, I haven't used a pencil since the fifth grade.* You don't have to, but I find the process works better if you do—and it might just take you back to a time when you dreamed a bit more than you do now.

Several years ago I stumbled upon the power of the pencil as I was in my home office, writing the outline for a talk I was preparing to give. I found myself scribbling, editing, and crossing things out with a pen. In the process, the paper became such a mess that it was distracting, keeping me from writing whatever was in my head. Frustrated with writer's block, I got up to get some water. In the kitchen, I saw a jar of pencils that my wife had for our kiddos' never-ending homework assignments. Blaming my pen for my problems, I decided to sharpen a pencil and see what would happen.

It helped.

I started on a fresh piece of paper, and I wrote. If I didn't like it, I erased it—and there wasn't any mess! My brain could finally start unloading on the paper. It was like a little piece of creative magic.

Writing in your own hand frees up your thinking in ways that typing on a computer doesn't. When you write something down, you're actually *in* the exercise, not just staring at it. Big difference.

I'll include plenty of follow-up questions for you if you get stuck, but answering the three Gift Indicator questions below is an eye-opener. It helps you see who you really are.

Also, remember: this isn't a quiz, so you can't fail. Sometimes we get so hung up on having the right answer that we shut ourselves down. If that's you, then start your sentence with, "If I had to guess, . . ." Then write what comes to mind, whatever it is. Give yourself permission to explore ideas and allow yourself the time you need to read your gauges. Sometimes we find the clues quickly; sometimes we have to search a while. The process works, so don't give up.

Talent Indicator: *What do you do best?* Identifying what you do best reveals your *talents*, spotlighting the job functions and skills you're especially good at. This includes your natural talents and trained skills

26

but also your people skills and character strengths. This last category is something that people often overlook, and yet we all use our personal strengths on the job every day. So make sure they're on your list!

Start with your hard skills—the tasks or roles that come easily to you and that colleagues, bosses, or customers have commended you for. These are job-specific abilities that make you proficient in your work and its processes, using the equipment and tools of your trade. Coding, presentation or language skills, certifications, spreadsheets, project management, or design are some examples.

Now list your soft skills—the personality or character traits that people recognize in you. They aren't unique to any job, but you use them on the job to succeed with people and to do your work better.[9] Decisiveness, empathy, humor, coachability, or optimism are just a few examples.

So, when you're at your best in the workplace, what do you do really well? Try to list at least five hard skills and soft skills. Now isn't the time to be humble. Take pride in what you excel at and write it down. When you're done, come right back to this page, and we'll keep going.

Here are some questions to help you get the brainstorm started:

- Where did I excel in school—what subject or activities?
- What task comes easily to me?
- What work or results do other people compliment me on?
- Am I better at relating with people, working with objects/my hands, or dealing with data/information?
- What's my unique contribution when I'm involved in a team project?

Passion Indicator: *What work do you love to do?* This is work you get excited just thinking about, the work that makes time disappear. The work that you get high emotion and devotion from—or, as I like to say, "It gives you the juice." What you love to do is important to clarify because the world is full of people who are really good at their job . . . but they can't stand it.

As you're reflecting on this question, focus your list on the responsibilities you'd do for free because you enjoy them that much. Shoot for a list of at least five.

Here are some more follow-up questions to help you figure out what you love to do:

- What kinds of work are you always excited to start?
- Which tasks engage you so much that time seems to disappear?
- Which work-related topics do you study up on during your free time (books, blogs, podcasts, etc.)?
- Which job duties do you wish were a bigger part of your day?
- If money were no object and you were guaranteed not to fail, what type of work would you do?

Mission Indicator: *What are the results of your work that matter deeply to you?* This is where your personal values become professional results. All work produces a result, and this question helps you identify the impact you want to make through your work.

Your mission addresses these concerns:

- Who are the people I want to help? *coachable who want + need help*
- What problem do they have?

- What do they need or want?
- Why do I feel connected to them?
- What solution do I most want to provide to them? *Listen*

You may have multiple answers for each of these concerns, but stay at this until you have a clear idea of your mission. Also, pay attention to the fact that mission is often deeply personal. Dave Ramsey built a company that helps people experience financial peace after he and his wife, Sharon, went bankrupt. I've heard more than one doctor say they went into their specialty because they lost someone they loved to that disease. My wife, Stacy, says it best: "Out of deep pain comes great passion." There's a reason something matters deeply to you—and it often informs the results you want to produce through your work.

Are you having fun with this question, or is it feeling really big and you're getting hung up? To get more specific, you can also ask:

- Which results from your past have mattered so deeply that they still make you proud to this day?
- How have you been able to help others in ways that were incredibly meaningful to you? The size of the task doesn't matter. How largely it affected your heart is the real indicator.
- Where do you volunteer? What causes inspire or deeply concern you?
- What have you done for the sake of others that you feel privileged to have been involved in? Something you've accomplished in your job may come to mind, but think beyond the workplace too.

- What have you participated in within your neighborhood or faith community, during your spare time, or as a hobby that has made someone else's life better and brightened your day?

Follow the Clues

With each of these three indicators, you're trying to follow the trail of clues. What patterns are emerging? Which key words make your heart jump a little? They're like footprints leading you in the direction of your purpose.

Now, all of this may seem like a lot to get clear on, but we're approaching it like a jigsaw puzzle. You've dumped all the pieces on the table and are sorting through them: first, collect all the blue pieces of the sky into a pile; then the brown pieces for the forest; then the green pieces for the pasture. As we connect the colors, and then connect those sections to each other, the whole picture comes to life.

Right now, you're still sorting out the colors. But they're about to start coming together.

Action 2: Get Feedback from Others

Once you've identified your talent, passion, and mission, go get some feedback on your answers. Why show somebody else what you've done? Two reasons: to make sure you're right and to make sure you haven't overlooked something about yourself that others see. No one would consider writing a book without an editor or releasing a drug without lab trials. Don't operate in a vacuum with your dream job either.

I'll never forget interviewing Jack Dorsey, cofounder of Twitter and CEO and cofounder of Square. He shared with me his methodology for evaluating new ideas, and for him, feedback is a priority. First, he draws it up to get it out of his head so he can "start criticizing it from a third-party perspective." If he still believes the idea has merit, he takes it to someone else and says, "Look, I think this is pretty interesting. What do you think?"

You can do the same as you explore who you are and what you were created to do. In life, it's almost impossible to get the full picture when we self-assess. Staring into a mirror, you only see your face. You don't see the bedhead you have going on in the back. Invite feedback from every angle and work to keep an open mind as you're receiving others' input. If the people you've consulted have your best interest at heart and really care about you, you can set aside your defenses and, as Dorsey put it, "allow [their feedback] to be an inspiration."[10]

Here's a bonus for following through on this step: you'll not only gain more clarity about what you do best, but you'll walk away from those conversations with more confidence. Feedback gives you clarity *and* confidence. It's a two-for-one deal.

My friend Derek experienced what can happen when you skip this step. A natural entrepreneur, he once had a big idea to start an organization built around an annual conference for young leaders. He was so gung-ho about it that he raced ahead without consulting anyone—not his friends or leaders of similar organizations. Had I known what he was thinking, I would have offered him one word: *Wait.* The idea had legs, but it wasn't ready—and neither was Derek. By the time I heard of his plans, he was already past the point of no return. He had filed the papers, picked a date, booked a venue, and launched a website.

He worked overtime to gather a small group of sponsors, exhibitors, and speakers. When the big day arrived, the event fell flat, and only a fraction of the attendees Derek had promised to sponsors showed up. The venue was far too large and sucked all the energy out of the room. Derek lost credibility with vendors and participants alike, and the organization folded under outstanding debts within a couple of years.

Looking back, Derek recognizes his mistakes, most of which could have been avoided if he had gotten feedback from others. Running your perceptions and dreams through credible filters can prevent a lot of wasted time and expense.[11]

Other people are often able to see us more clearly than we can see ourselves. So arrange to sit down with three or four people who know you well and discuss your responses with them. If they see the same talents, passions, and mission as you, you'll know you're headed in the right direction.

Action 3: Draft a Purpose Statement

Once you have the clear "data" on your talent, passion, and mission, you're ready to plug that information in to create your very own purpose statement. This purpose statement will help you answer, "What should I do with my life?"

To get clear on this, take your confirmed talents, passions, and mission and drop them in to complete this sentence:

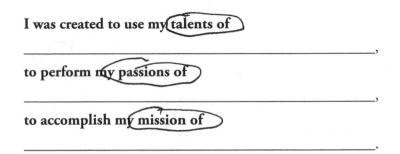

I was created to use my talents of

_____,

to perform my passions of

_____,

to accomplish my mission of

_____.

Here are a couple of examples:

Jerome:

I was created to use my talents of **inspection, organization,** and **execution,** to perform my passions of **analyzing, planning,** and **finishing,** to accomplish my mission of **solution** by producing fixes and systems.

Adriane:

I was created to use my talents of **communication, discernment,** and **persuasion,** to perform my passions of **advising, leading,** and **teaching,** to accomplish my mission of **influence** by producing change and progress.

This exercise will alert you to how clear you are about who you are. If you read this summary statement and you're not feeling it—if something about your talent, your passion, or your mission doesn't absolutely fire you up—then go back to the process for that part of the puzzle and find the missing piece. I went through plenty of trial and error before I found my unique role. If you want to be guided through this exercise, you can take my Get Clear Career Assessment at ramseysolutions.com/getclear. It will write your purpose statement for you and accelerate your self-awareness so you can identify what you were born to do and where you want to do it.

Action 4: Find Your Marketplace Matches

Now look back over the purpose statement you've just assembled. Picture in your mind the vast marketplace made up of sectors, industries, careers, and jobs, and ask yourself: How and where can I use what I do best, to perform the work I love most, to produce the results that matter to me?

The answer is probably in multiple jobs and on multiple career paths. Filling your unique role in the workplace means you're in your sweet spot, like we talked about in chapter 1. You're operating *at the intersection of your talents, passions, and mission*—working *on purpose*—and you not only know it, but you feel it.

Possibilities are good at this point. Every industry, every field, has various jobs and careers available. Focus on identifying several career paths you can explore that you believe fit your unique role.

For example, I talked with a high school student, Caitlyn, not so long ago who wanted to be a nurse—she just wasn't sure what type of nurse. After all, just like doctors, nurses can specialize in any number of fields: some work the admitting room or the emergency room; others love the operating room or physical rehab; and still others serve in geriatrics, intensive care, or the delivery room. And, of course, there are dozens of places where a nursing degree can be put to use beyond a hospital, including retirement centers, schools, or addiction recovery facilities.

Some preliminary online research will tell Caitlyn what those specialties are and what general qualifications she needs to move forward. Between that front-end information and her own self-awareness, she's going to decide that most of those seeming "matches" are only a partial fit, and she'll eliminate them from her search.

If she discovers, for instance, that she's not cut out to be an ER nurse, that's not a failure—that's clarity working for her! It's a clear no for her, and she's not confused. She's one step closer to her yes. Medical doctors explore various areas of medicine during their rotations to find out which fits them best. Why not the rest of us?

As you're exploring potential matches, don't worry if you seem to be saying, "No. Next!" a lot. That's okay. Whatever you eliminate and whatever you keep at this stage, your research has done its work.

This is the most exciting part of the Get Clear stage to me. Once you identify jobs and career paths that are in your sweet spot, you've set yourself free! The pressure's off. No more worries that you missed THE perfect job. No more tossing and turning at night about having chosen the wrong career. Your sweet spot includes multiple career paths and many jobs that you will love.

Action 5: Verify Your Dream Job

In this final step, it's time to verify what you have clarified. By *verify*, I mean learning more, researching each of your best matches in depth.

In doing that, you'll be able to decide one by one: "Yes, it's a match" or "No, it's not."

I told Caitlyn, "Every moment you're not in class, you need to be shadowing a nurse or having coffee with a nurse. You need to get as much information as you can about the different types of nursing professions and what each one is really like. Clarify the ones that interest you, toss the ones that don't, and ultimately, you'll verify one that fits you like a glove. Then you can figure out what you need to do to get that job."

Once you find the roles that are strong possibilities, you're going to do some deeper research. First, dive in online and get all the facts you can, including salary ranges and job availability. Second, you must talk to the experts—the people who are doing those jobs every day—to get beneath the surface and learn what's really involved. Essentially, you're doing a deep dive on every profession that intrigues you: What was each person's career path? Their background? How did they get hired? What programs or training did they need? Also, what is their day-to-day experience: What are the hours? The chances of being promoted? Gather all the pros and cons you can find. Find out what they love about their job—but also learn what's hard about it and what frustrates them.

The most important part of verifying your dream job is that both your heart and your head must say yes without reservation. Knowing a job makes logical sense—"It will pay well" or "This industry is practically layoff-proof"—is good, but logic isn't enough to get clear. Your head can't have the only say, and neither can your heart. They have to be in full agreement.

Choose a job at this stage that is all head and you'll be like the many people who have called in to my show, desperate for change and full of regret for making the "safe choice." Make an all-heart choice—"Ahhh, it'd be so great to have my own business" or "That sounds so cool!"— and you'll be calling me in a year because the honeymoon is over and you're brokenhearted and depressed.

Don't rely solely on the stats and salaries, and don't rely on your romantic view of the work. Talk to people and check the facts. The more you learn, the more you'll know for sure whether this prospect is a long-lasting "marriage" or not and whether your heart and your head are 100 percent in it or not.

Want an example? On the surface, a lot of people are in love with the idea of owning a vineyard. I'll admit, Vineyard Owner is a nice title. But remember, you're looking past the title and exploring the actual job description for compatibility with who you are and the type of work you need.

My friend Jennifer and her family have actually owned and run a vineyard, and it involves a lot of work that somebody might not find so appealing once they scratch the surface. She says,

> When people find out I used to live on a vineyard, they start gushing about how amazing and wonderful it must have been. They're picturing Napa Valley at sunset, sitting on a magnificently landscaped patio with a glass of wine in hand, and I just shake my head because they have no idea.
>
> They have no idea that we worked seventeen hours a day, seven days a week, in the Texas heat. That my family and I

smelled like cow manure because that's what we spread as fertilizer. That we had to wear chaps to fend off rattlesnakes and carry pistols to protect ourselves from feral hogs. That our equipment broke down regularly, and fixing it cost tens of thousands of dollars. They have no clue about how hard it is. And that's why you need to do your research—because romantic notions will eat you for lunch.

For most of us, after about two sentences of a vineyard owner's day-to-day realities, we would've said, "See ya! I'm out!" For a rare few folks, however, those hard realities sound more like a labor of love than a hardship. Maybe you grew up on a farm, and you know for a fact that you don't mind the long hours, the funky smells, the sunburn, or the snakes. In fact, you'd take that any day over being surrounded by four walls, enduring mind-numbing meetings, and watching the clock tick by one hour at a time. To you, an office job would be torture.

That's how you know your heart is all in: when you've learned the bad and the ugly and you're still willing to suffer for it because the good is amazing. That's your passion and your purpose speaking—your heart and your head—and those are the parts of you that give you endurance. The training, the heat, the hard work, the day-to-day setbacks? You endure them all and still, you're energized. Why? Because you love the work and you're working toward your dream!

But let's say you've done all this clarifying and verifying . . . and three dream jobs are still staring at you. What then?

At the end of the day, it comes down to the heart test. I'm about to challenge you the way I do callers to the show because we get this all the time. Close your eyes and tell me, "If you could choose only one of them—A, B, or C—which one is it? If you were guaranteed to be successful in all three but had to pick just one, what does your heart want?"

Almost every time, it's A. That's the one that's been begging both your heart and your mind, "Pick me!"

The truth is, you were never actually unclear about which job you wanted most. You were *afraid of picking the wrong one.*

This process works every time. Not just for getting clear on which dream job to pursue, but to clarify virtually any aspect of your career. The simple but powerful process of "clarify and verify" is what allows you to avoid analysis paralysis and keep moving forward.

Remember to Revisit Clarity

If you're reading this and you've done the work, then I assume you've had your "big reveal." All the evidence is in, and you have your winner. That's a huge deal, and I'm super proud of you! You've done what few people in this world ever do.

Be sure to celebrate this moment in your own way. Maybe you journal about it, call a close family member or friend, or post a celebration video on social media. (Just remember not to ruin your reputation!)

Also, as you continue on this journey to your dream, keep in mind that you can revisit the Get Clear stage as often as necessary. Remember freeze tag as a kid? You knew there was always a home base so you had a safe place to go to catch your breath.

Getting clear is home base. The minute fear or confusion comes your way? Turn back to clarity. You were laid off? Come back to clarity.

You got what you thought was your dream job, but it's in a toxic environment? Don't get discouraged—dive back into clarity.

Life is going to take you on detours. Financial issues, relationship problems, or illness can rock your world. Circumstances will fog your vision and cause confusion. You'll still be okay because you've learned how to get clear. And knowing you can retreat to clarity at any time means, no matter what comes at you, you'll be able to get up, dust yourself off, and find the path back to your sweet spot.

Now that you know what you want to do, it's time to move on to Stage 2, Get Qualified, where you'll earn your ticket to get on the track to your dream job.

Chapter 2 Takeaways

Remember This
You already have the answers you need to get clear.

You Got This
All that's required is for you to be true to who you are.

Do This
Complete the five actions in this chapter to get
clear on what you were made to do.

STAGE 2

Get Qualified for the Work You Want to Do

3

The Four Questions to Get You in the Door

I was so excited when I got the phone call.

This was my first real break toward my dream job . . . or so I thought. I'd only just discovered that broadcasting was the path for me. I knew I loved sports. I knew I *loved* performing. And I lived in Atlanta, home to Turner Broadcasting System and Turner Sports. For someone who wanted to break into national broadcasting but not relocate, this was my best shot.

Having been in Atlanta for several years, I'd worked my connections and got an email introduction to an on-air talent at Turner Sports. That email turned into a scheduled phone call. I had worked very hard to make this conversation happen and was so excited that I had to take a deep breath before answering the call.

After a few minutes of small talk, he asked if I had a demo tape. My excitement immediately turned into embarrassment. *I was humiliated!* I didn't have one, of course, because I had not actually done any broadcasting work, ever. I hurriedly assured him that I had the raw talent and would come do a demo for him in person if he'd let me. I now know that never happens, but I was so clueless that my request either came off as confident or he had compassion for my cluelessness and felt bad for me. It was probably the latter. But it worked. So after his NASCAR show one day, he had his television crew stay and he gave me a shot at doing one of the highlights packages he had just done on his show.

Now keep in mind, people, I'd never done sports TV—ever. I'd never been live on television for even one second. This fact had escaped me until the moment I got behind the desk and looked at the hungry and tired crew who was ready to go home.

There are no words to describe the level of anxiety I had. My mouth was so dry my lips wouldn't open.

After a two-minute lesson on what he wanted me to do, the host asked the crew if they were ready, then looked at me and said, "Let's go in 5, 4, 3, 2, 1 . . . Action!" Instantly the red light on the camera lit up, and the teleprompter started scrolling. It's all in a day's work for someone who has bothered to get qualified. But me? When my big moment came, I choked, hard. And not on my saliva—I didn't have any to choke on.

The teleprompter was rolling, and I couldn't keep up. My vision blurred. My words got all twisted. I kept stuttering and took breaths at all the wrong times. My delivery couldn't have been worse. This was my shot and I was *so. not. ready.* I completely blew it. It was gut-wrenching. Still is. I am experiencing anxiety as I write this.

After the train wreck was over, he told me to relax and try it again. I'm not sure what I did next could be described as trying, but after two more takes, the guy finally put me out of my misery.

"Okay, we're done," he told his crew. And so was I.

When the crew left, he looked at me like, "Really, dude? You talked me into this?" I was defeated. I was exposed as a fraud in front of an industry veteran.

That excruciating experience was the day I learned one of the most important lessons about getting to your dream job: You've got to get qualified *the right way*. You've got to earn it.

Just as there are no shortcuts to paying off debt and saving for retirement, there are no shortcuts to your dream job. Why? There's a lot to be learned, a lot to be done—and it's going to take time.

Price of Admission

Frankly, no matter who you are or how old you are, almost no one is prepared for their dream job coming off of Stage 1. I don't say that to discourage you, but to help you see that there's a gap between where you are today and where you need to be in order to succeed in your sweet spot.

And that gap comes with a lot of questions:

Who can ever afford to make the switch?

Will I be able to do the job once I'm qualified?

How can I hope to catch up when I'm already behind everybody else my age?

This is the nature of Stage 2. It's marked by uncertainty.

For that reason, getting qualified might not be your favorite stage. There's a lot of time and sheer sacrifice involved—a lot of earning your stripes and hustling day after day . . . often for years. But it's a powerful

45

stage too because this is where momentum meets you. This is where you begin to make progress toward your dream.

During Stage 2, you may feel anxiety. You may lack confidence. You may be short on courage or grow impatient. That's normal! There's nothing wrong with you. Those feelings are signs that this journey matters to you and that you are invested.

Thankfully, getting qualified isn't super complicated. You *can* learn how to successfully make the climb and reach the peak. It's all about creating a great plan, and in this chapter I'll show you how.

We're going to walk through four questions that will help you develop your plan to get qualified. By the time we're finished, your professional pinnacle will be looking very achievable.

Four Qualifying Questions

One of the greatest fears we have is of the unknown. In this context, how to get qualified can seem scary because you don't have the knowledge to answer that question. So over the next several pages, we're going to design your plan for reaching the peak by answering four questions. Your answers will qualify you for the climb by addressing the biggest unknowns:

1. The Education Question: What do I need to learn?
2. The Experience Question: What do I need to do?
3. The Economic Question: How much will it cost?
4. The Expectation Question: How long will it take?

Each one builds on the next, so work through them one at a time, in the order they're presented.

The Education Question: *What do I need to learn?*

The first question you need to ask is what know-how and skills will get you to the goal. The answer used to be: go to college and get a degree. Today? Maybe not.

There's still an underlying belief in certain communities, and very often in families, that college is *the* path to the dream. Even now, most parents want their kids to get a degree because they think it's the best chance for career success. The data, though, offers a wider picture. Check out these statistics:

- The Federal Reserve Bank of New York reports that over 40 percent of college grads are working a job that doesn't need a degree.[12]
- As of 2019, the employment rate of twenty-five to thirty-four-year-olds with no college education was around 74 percent, while the employment rate of college-educated people in the same age group was only a little higher, around 87 percent.[13]

So don't assume you need a college diploma. While a degree is sometimes required, more and more employers, including some of America's largest companies, no longer require a bachelor's degree for many of their job listings. They've decided that worker skills matter more. So be sure to find out if you really need the degree.

With the average tuition for a year of college ranging anywhere from $10,000 for a public, in-state university to $50,000 for a private university, this one decision could save you a huge amount of time and money. Even if you can't skip the degree, you can for sure skip the outrageous cost of a name-brand school. Nobody in the workplace actually cares where you went to school. How do I know? When was the last time you asked your doctor to show you their diploma before an appointment? What matters is getting the training to be able to do the job you love. That's all. Stop caring what everybody else thinks and start focusing on getting where you want to be!

For jobs that don't require a four-year degree, alternatives such as trade schools, community colleges, certification programs, apprenticeships, the military, or entrepreneurship may be your route to getting the knowledge you need for the job you want. Think of it: while your friends are studying about their field in college, you could already have two or three years of real experience in your dream industry *and* be accomplishing your savings and investment goals.

Todd took the trade-school route. He attended welding school two days a week—combining classroom learning and hands-on practice—and then spent three days per week in a welding shop, where he gained on-the-job training. A year later, after completing the program, his starting salary was $50,000 a year.

That's how much the business world has changed. Instead of one primary route to your dream job, now you have up to three, depending on the profession:

1. Traditional Education
2. Certification (alternative or shorter-term programs)
3. Workification (my word for learning and earning in the workplace). This is what I did. I don't have a degree—I worked my way

into broadcasting. Companies are doing more and more training through apprenticeships, internships, and other job programs.

So when someone asks me, "Should I go to school?"—whether it's a high school student weighing their options or someone older who is wanting to change careers—my answer is this: If higher education is not the *only* way or the *best* way, don't do it! Use that time and money on the qualifications you actually need.

There are a variety of ways to get the knowledge you need without getting a traditional degree:

- Online tutorials
- Job shadowing
- Internships
- Microdegrees
- Auditing college courses
- Books
- Massive open online courses, known as MOOCs. Examples: Udemy, Udacity, edX, Saylor Academy, Coursera, Harvard Free Online Courses, Open Yale Courses
- Webinars
- Podcasts

You need knowledge and training to get qualified, without question. Just don't assume there's only one way to get it. Clarify and verify the amount and type of knowledge you need to be hired into your dream industry, and then choose the best route for getting there.

The Experience Question: *What do I need to do?*

This question is asking what level of experience you need to get hired.

For me, I knew I would never be able to do a national radio show until I proved I could do a local one. So I did a local broadcast on Saturdays. I was terrible, but the whole point was to learn and get better. I needed to learn, for example, how to develop and deliver content in eight minutes or less, how to do short interviews that still packed in a lot of information for listeners, and how to watch a clock but not be distracted by it. With time and practice, I got a little better, and eventually, I was given the opportunity to do a show five days a week.

Probably the best advice I can give you right now is to *be patient with yourself.* The way Dave Ramsey says it is: "Embrace the suck." Everybody expects you to suck at what you do when you're first starting out. Though it may be a while before you excel at your role, keep at it. You'll get better.

I know it's not fun to be at the low end of the learning curve. Especially in an entry-level position, you can feel like nobody's seeing you and nothing's happening. You might be deeply frustrated like Daniel-san in the movie *The Karate Kid.* He wanted to learn karate, and his teacher, Mr. Miyagi, taught him by instructing him to paint Miyagi's fence and wax his car. It didn't make any sense! But what Daniel didn't know was that showing up every day to do these menial tasks was giving him hours of batting practice. He was actually learning the fundamentals and practicing the moves so that one day he could fight and win. Be patient as you gain experience—put in the hours each step of the way so you can earn the next opportunity.

Christine was putting the hours in while she worked full time at her day job—a job that offered no stability and caused constant worry. Thankfully, she'd already identified her passion—a wedding photography business—and she'd been shooting weddings for a few months now. But how could she transition her passion into a career?

For her to get qualified, she needed to keep shooting weddings along with other types of events like family reunions, birthday parties, retirement parties, and engagements. This is also a field where it's easy to get more training through YouTube videos and local classes. Taking every opportunity to build her portfolio would give her the experience she needed to one day take the leap and make this her career.

Then there's Ben, who asked a question a lot of people have. He wrote: "Ken, I'm in school to get my degree in accounting. I have about a year left. I was looking at job ads in that field. Everyone is asking for experience. How do I get experience when most are requiring two years in order to start?"

This is where a lot of people get locked up. They see the two-year requirement and mentally disqualify themselves. Do you know the reason companies say this? Because they don't want people who aren't qualified.

Ben can get qualified, and even rack up the hours to match—he just won't be doing it the traditional way.

What do I mean? How can anyone accumulate two years of experience without spending two years in one job?

First, *use the advantages you do have.* In Ben's case, he has the freedom that a full-time employee doesn't. He can fill in at one or more accounting businesses during every school break over the next year and during his entire summer break. His dad runs some businesses too. Ben could do bookkeeping for his dad all year long. He could also check with the accounting department at his school and offer to give them some hours between classes.

Second, *look for side jobs within your field that don't require two years of experience.* You need to get the job that gets you the experience to get the job you want. Read that again, slowly. I'll put in commas this time to help: You need to get the job, that gets you the experience, to get the job you want. There's a reason these jobs are called entry level. They allow you to *enter* the field.

Besides part-time accounting jobs for established businesses, Ben could step out on his own and offer basic accounting help to small businesses or churches, even if it's just ten hours a week. Were he to secure two, maybe three, part-time clients, the multiplied efforts would help him accumulate the hours of experience he needs for his resumé, plus make him a little money. And those clients might serve as references for him in the future, or even hire him once he graduates.

Third, *find another way.* Anyone can gain experience by volunteering. Nonprofits in particular are interested in hiring *you*, not your experience. They need good, hands-on help. What if Ben volunteered to help a local nonprofit with their bookkeeping a couple of evenings a week or every Saturday until he graduates?

There is always a way if you look for it.

The Economic Question: *How much will it cost?*

After determining what type of education and experience you need to get qualified, you need to find out how much doing these things will cost. Keep in mind that this question isn't just about finances. You're finding out: How much money will I need to save? *and* How much time will I need to sacrifice in my schedule?

Before you start climbing toward your professional summit, you need to know how much money it's going to take. How much will your education cost? Will you need to volunteer or take a pay cut to gain experience? How will you need to adjust your monthly budget? While getting qualified will likely cost you—it may not cost as much as you think.

Let's look at Jacob as an example. He took a lot of detours before finding his dream job as an app developer. To get qualified, he first earned an online associate degree for mobile applications development—only to find that it got him nowhere. He couldn't even get an interview for a tech position! Then he heard about a company that offered courses focused on technical skills development, many of them for free. The company partners with large tech companies like Amazon, Google, and Uber to develop training courses in specific skills that these businesses need. These companies then headhunt from that pool of alumni.

Jacob's "nanodegree" (a certificate-type program, usually for tech roles) only cost him $500. He said he learned more in that brief program than he did in eighteen months in a college classroom. He also received career-skills training that helped him craft his resumé and learn the language he needed to nail his interviews. A few months after completing his coursework, Jacob started his new job as a mobile app developer.

In the Education Question we discussed previously, I listed nine ways to get the knowledge you need, besides a college degree. Every one of those options costs less than pursuing a degree—and several of them cost nothing. If getting qualified means going to school, explore *all* of your options.

As you consider how much it will cost you to get qualified, resist the temptation to take on debt. Most people will tell you borrowing money for your education is a smart decision for your future. They say it's an investment in yourself, but don't buy it! Taking on debt doesn't help you rise to the challenge—it takes you further away from your dream. Think about it: in order to get qualified, you need flexibility. You may need to take a lower-paying job that's in your new field. But if you're taking out thousands of dollars in debt, you're going to need to make *more* money to cover those payments, not less. Paying cash to get qualified is the fastest—and smartest—way to your dream job.

For some of you, the financial aspect of "How much will it cost?" will hit you like a wrecking ball to the chest. You might be living paycheck to paycheck without a plan for your money, let alone any savings. You might be drowning in debt. You might be in survival mode after being laid off with no warning. And just the thought of having to cover your rent or mortgage this month causes your heart rate to spike. If this is you, first take a deep breath. I know what it's like to be where you are. *You will get through this.*

Second, if your money is a mess, take control of that starting today. You need to do a monthly budget. You need to have an emergency fund and get out of debt. If this is all foreign to you, check out Ramsey+ at ramseyplus.com. It includes Financial Peace University and the world's best budgeting tool to help you pay off debt faster. Once you're in control of your money, you'll be in a position to make the decisions—and the sacrifices—to reach your goal.

It might feel like a delay to do this. But really, it's setting you up for financial peace and the freedom to go after your dreams. It's like when you have a knee injury. You can't get in top shape when your meniscus needs to be repaired. Get that done, then you can get to work achieving the dream.

Also, even if you do need to clean up your finances, get the answers to "How much will it cost?" anyway. That way you can make a plan—and you may be able to start sooner than you think. And always remember that starting small is still starting. Community college or online education are great ways to cover the basics without breaking the bank. If you can only afford to take one class, then do that. It's still moving forward. Don't let "I can't do the entire program right now" become an excuse. Do what you can. *Any progress is still progress.*

The other type of cost you'll encounter on this journey is giving up your time. Getting qualified is going to mean making some trade-offs. Your bandwidth is going to be limited. You'll have less time for the people you love and the hobbies you enjoy. Saying yes to getting qualified means saying no to something or someone else.

There were many, many times while getting qualified that I thought to myself, *Man, I don't have time for this!* While I was trying to gain the experience I needed, my wife, Stacy, and I had three kids under the age of three. It was so intense that at night I dreamed—I mean, had nightmares—of changing diapers. Plus, I was running a business and trying to get a radio show off the ground. I never felt like I really had time, but I learned I had to make the time. It was now or never for me.

How do you make time when you feel like you don't have it? You borrow it from other places in your life. For instance, I stopped playing golf and going to poker nights with my buddies. I also watched a lot less TV.

I've never met anyone who couldn't reallocate at least a few hours a week. I'm not suggesting that you neglect your spouse or your children. I'm saying, sacrifice the lesser stuff: Get off social media. Change your workout schedule. Skip a season of your favorite show. Pay a neighbor kid (or your own kid!) to mow your lawn all summer long so you don't have to. These small deposits—an hour here, two hours there—can quickly add up toward getting qualified faster.

Making time *work for you* is a key to making progress at this stage. You may not have a ton of resources or money, but you do have twenty-four hours each day. And your time is your single greatest investment in your future. Use it to your advantage.

Julie's challenge was how to juggle both her time and her finances. She was willing to make the sacrifice—she just wasn't clear on how to make it work.

She had recently earned her bachelor's in business and biology. She knew her sweet spot was working with animals in either a zoo or an aquarium, and her passion was educating the public on how to better protect animals and the environment.

When Julie and I talked, she was working full time at a call center just to pay the bills. Like many college grads, she had a lot of student loan debt, and she needed to make at least $40,000 a year to cover living expenses and pay down that debt.

While the call-center job provided the salary she needed, she was working from noon to nine o'clock at night—the same times that zoos and aquariums are typically open. And those sweet-spot jobs she'd identified only paid about nine dollars per hour to start, an enormous pay cut that she would need to address.

After looking at her options, Julie realized the solution was shifting her schedule. At her age, and while she was still single, she had the freedom to work a more unusual schedule. So we brainstormed some ideas: Perhaps she could switch to a nighttime shift at the call center and work at the zoo during the day. Or maybe she could pursue the zoo job to get the gig and then supplement her income with a second, part-time job.

Single or married, working a second job is a good choice for many people. According to the US Bureau of Labor Statistics, approximately 4 percent of employed American adults have more than one job.[14] That's nearly eight million people.[15] Yes, it's an enormous sacrifice, but it's not permanent. A lot of men and women find they have the capacity to do it *because* it's only temporary. Be willing to adjust your schedule and tighten your finances for a season if that's what you need to do to get qualified.

The Expectation Question: How long will it take?

This last question to consider is the timeline question. What's realistic? Should you expect it to take months, a year, several years?

When I ask people, "Are you willing to do what it takes to get your dream job?" their answer is always: "Sure, sure!" But when I ask them, "Are you willing to wait as long as you have to?" I often hear crickets.

Everybody's all in for the dream as long as it happens on their timeline. But if it takes longer than they hoped? That's the real test. In those times, you have to do a gut check. You have to dig in and want it even more than you did when everything was sunshine and butterflies.

From the get-go here, you need to make two words your mantra: *No shortcuts.* In college, you take the general education stuff before you can study the good stuff in your major. Why should it be any different for a pursuit as important as your career?

No one ever says "I'm going to scale Mount Everest" one day and then hops a plane to Tibet the next. This is a marathon, not a hundred-meter sprint. When you're doing something this big and worthwhile, endurance is everything.

Once I decided to pursue broadcasting in 2005, I asked my wife, "Are you all in?"

She was.

I added, "I want you to know it may take five to seven years."

Famous last words.

It took nearly seven years before I joined Ramsey Solutions, and my big break there wasn't until 2017—three years after they hired me. So, ten years to the dream job, start to finish.

Certain industries are more predictable than broadcasting, and not everybody has nearly the climb that I did. Some of you already have experience in your chosen career. But in any line of work, the timeline can change at a moment's notice because of an injury, an illness in the family, a layoff. Avalanches like these knock people off their feet every day. So tack on some extra time in your mind to keep your impatience from sabotaging you. It almost always takes longer than you expect. And impatience, like debt, doesn't get you to the goal sooner—it causes reckless decisions that set you back.

None of us wants to go slow. But getting qualified is the foundation you're building your career on. Don't shortchange yourself.

A Plan You Can Act On

You know what I did after my humiliating demo that day at the Turner Sports studio? I signed up for a broadcasting class with a bunch of college students. Me, the thirty-something dad of three, learning alongside ten people who were half my age. Yet that's exactly what I needed. That's where I learned how to perform my craft in front of a microphone—learning and earning.

The reward is worth all the work. So take your time formulating your answers to these qualifying questions. You're creating a plan to prepare for your climb, and you're building up the kind of confidence that only comes from riding out the learning curve the right way.

Once you're done with these questions, there's one other thing you need in order to get completely qualified. We'll cover that in chapter 4.

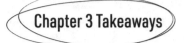

Chapter 3 Takeaways

Remember This
Getting qualified isn't overwhelming if you have a plan.

You Got This
Be patient. Your time will come.

Do This
Answer the four qualifying questions and make a plan to get qualified.

4

The Secret to Sticking with It

Elite athletes do a lot of things that others don't. In the 1980s, researchers stumbled upon something called "the quiet eye" as they measured where and how long athletes *looked* as they performed. What they discovered is that just before they made a move, these athletes held their gaze longer than their lesser competitors. In other words, *they focused longer than anyone else.*

Serena Williams, who has won twenty-three Grand Slam singles titles in tennis, says it like this: "If you're behind in a game, it's so important to relax, and that's what I do. . . . Focus on one point at a time . . . just focus on that sole point, and then the next one, and the next one, only as they come."[16] She's not looking around at the fans cheering her on during the match. She doesn't stop to think about the sweat running down her forehead. She's not considering where she's going for takeout that night. She's intently focused in the present moment on that one point. She fixes her gaze and doesn't allow any distraction to derail her. Period.

Here's the thing most people don't expect about getting qualified: the biggest threat to your success in Stage 2 isn't that others will disqualify you, *it's that you'll disqualify yourself.* You can get distracted. Your focus can waver. And you miss the point. Let me explain.

At some point on this journey, you will face distraction. One or more of the following will happen:

- You won't get the job you want.
- Someone will tell you that you don't have what it takes.
- You'll take a serious financial hit.
- You'll have a toxic boss.
- You won't be good at something you're supposed to be good at.
- You'll straight-up fail at something.
- You'll be terrified you can't do the job.

When this happens, you're going to face a moment when you must choose where to fix your gaze—on your dream or the distraction. Most people let their focus slip. They get discouraged. They start worrying and thinking endlessly about worst-case scenarios. And they wind up completely bailing on their dream.

Your success in getting qualified—as well as in achieving your dream job—is a direct result of your ability to focus longer than everybody else. You're either going to put your mind to work for you, or you'll let it sabotage everything you're working toward. That's why part of Stage 2 is training your mind for the climb. In this chapter, I'll show you how to make your mind your greatest ally.

Step 1: Set Realistic Expectations

"I'm pregnant!"

Tears were streaming down her face as my wife, Stacy, waved the pregnancy test in front of me.

I just stood there, wide-eyed and in shock, trying to take it all in. Don't get me wrong: I was over-the-moon excited, but never in a million years did I see this coming.

After years of infertility, Stacy and I had known the joy of adding to our family through adoption. Ty was two and a half, and just fourteen days earlier, we'd brought home our second son, Chase, who was a newborn. We already had two children, ages two and under. Absorbing the fact that we would soon have a third was overwhelming. Little did I know that was just the first wild and crazy turn we would experience.

We were caught off guard again when morning sickness hit Stacy . . . *hard.* So hard she couldn't even stand up without feeling nauseated, let alone take care of our two young boys. We immediately had to hire help to care for the boys during the day, and I was on full-time dad duty every night. It rocked our world for six months, and then Stacy went to her regularly scheduled late-term checkup.

At her checkup, the doctor discovered that Stacy was leaking amniotic fluid. Instead of a late December delivery, first thing in the morning on December 2, we were at the hospital for an emergency C-section. We had no idea baby Josie's birth would play out as it did. It was both sooner and scarier than we expected.

Whether it's your life or your career, it's just not always going to turn out like you hope. The unexpected will happen. You may get blindsided or treated unfairly. But if you will set your expectations correctly up front, it will change the way you experience challenges and hardship. How do you do this? By *setting realistic expectations.*

You heard me. Set *realistic* expectations. Not great ones or poor ones. Nothing overly optimistic, yet no doom and gloom either. Your path to meaningful work isn't an all-inclusive cruise where everything is arranged in advance and follows a set schedule. No one's telling you what's ahead and how to dress.

The path to your dream job is an expedition. You have to pack and prepare for the likeliest scenarios and then improvise as you go—just like Stacy and I had to do in the days leading up to Josie's birth. In certain ways, the journey to getting qualified might be easier than you think. In other ways, it could be harder. You have to understand that as you're setting out.

Realistic expectations actually make you stronger. They cushion the blow when the unexpected happens. And they give you extra stamina when things don't go as you hoped. This makes you less vulnerable to discouragement and defeat and less likely to bail completely on your dream. Let's take a look at a couple of ways to set realistic expectations.

Assume There Are Challenges Ahead

Set realistic expectations by assuming you'll face some hazards. This is basic, but you might be surprised by the number of people—especially younger people—who don't start with this mindset. They assume that if they're doing the right thing, it will be easy, that they'll never face rejection or failure. And then when they hit a roadblock, it sends them into a tailspin. They start doubting their abilities, their path, and their sweet spot.

Listen, it's important to be positive, but there's a difference between positive and naïve. Encountering a setback doesn't mean you chose the wrong path—it means you're attempting something. It happens to all of us! When you assume you *will* face challenges, you prevent your emotions from getting the best of you and stay focused on the path ahead.

Think of all those students who had internships lined up for the summer of 2020, and then COVID-19 hit. What about the thousands of employees who were furloughed? Could anyone have imagined something as severe as a pandemic? Nope. But allowing for the possibility that an internship might not work out or that you could lose your job? Sure, those are real risks, even without a global pandemic. If you simply expect some roadblocks along the way, you'll be able to maintain your focus more easily. And you'll also be able to face them with more flexibility and positivity when they happen.

Learn What to Expect in Your Field and Prepare for the Likeliest Possibilities

The second way to set realistic expectations is to talk to people in your line of work. Go to those who have walked many miles on the path you're wanting to take and ask them:

- In what ways was getting qualified different than you thought it would be?
- How was it harder than you imagined?

I can promise they'll have stories and good counsel in each category.

Once you've heard from the industry pros, take what you learned and play out potential scenarios ahead of time. Develop some plan Bs based on what you've been told to expect. Also, knowing yourself and your circumstances as you do, predict where disruptions to your plan are most likely to occur. What can you do now to give yourself some peace of mind? How can you build in some cushion, just in case?

A teammate of mine shared with me her experience when she discovered she was pregnant for the first time. She was intent on a natural birth and preparing accordingly, but one of her friends—an RN in the NICU at a large hospital—gave her some very practical advice: "Jessica, just for a few days, I want you to research and own the possibility that you might need an emergency cesarean section. Find out what to expect and what choices you'll have. Play it out in your mind. Decide if you want your husband to stay with you or go with the baby if she's taken away. That way, if something unexpected does happen, you'll have a game plan."

Jessica didn't end up having a cesarean, but she did have a long, hard delivery that took several unexpected turns. Because she had done the research beforehand though, she was far more calm and confident as her daughter's birth unfolded. The same can be true as you play out potential plan Bs while you're getting qualified.

With some contingency plans in place, you won't need to overreact or get locked up. You'll be prepared to control what you can and adjust what you must.

Step 2: Choose Your Focus

Once you've set realistic expectations, take the next step to train your mind to expect and overcome challenges. The second step is to *intentionally choose your focus*.

Our focus is nothing short of a built-in superpower—but we don't think of it that way. In fact, we usually don't think about our focus at all. And that's the problem.

By intentionally deciding what to focus on, you and your brain become almost unstoppable! Because . . .

What you focus on is what you act on.

Thoughts produce actions! Where your sights go, you go. What you pay attention to will predict your performance.

This is due to a pencil-thin bundle of neurons at the base of your brain, just above your spinal cord, where the Reticular Activating System (RAS) lives. It's the attention center of your brain, and it empowers you to literally turn your attention to one thing and completely away from another.[17] I'll apply it to getting qualified in a minute, but first, let's dive in to a little brain science to understand how it works in everyday life.

The RAS is the filter between your subconscious and your conscious brain. Your subconscious brain spends all day, every day quietly taking in the massive amounts of information that come at your senses. Because your conscious brain can only pay attention to a few things at any one time, your RAS, in effect, acts as the conscious brain's "nightclub bouncer."[18] But you're still the boss—the RAS only does what *you* tell it to. So every time you decide that something is worth your attention, you've basically informed your Reticular Activating System: "If this thing shows up, tell me, and let it in." You're also saying, "Don't bother me if it's not on the 'guest list.'"

Want an example? Have you ever wondered why you start seeing cars like yours *everywhere* after you've just bought a car? Obviously the whole world didn't go out and purchase your vehicle overnight. What's changed is your focus. That's the RAS at work. You're now seeing those other cars because they have meaning to you they didn't have before. Your Reticular Activating System always ignored those vehicles until you owned one yourself. As one writer put it: "It filters the world through the parameters you give it. . . . The RAS helps you see what you want to see and in doing so, influences your actions."[19]

Your RAS also helps you hear what you want to hear. That's how you're able to hear your name above a crowd. It's also why your baby's panicked cry wakes you up in the middle of the night, but your spouse's snores don't. The RAS is always on alert and always paying attention to the things in your environment that you've put on the radar and classified as IMPORTANT.

Scientists have repeated a pretty funny experiment over the years that proves how well the RAS weeds out everything but what we're focused on. This video experiment records two teams of three students each, weaving among each other and passing a basketball. The instructions to the test subjects are simple: count how many times the team wearing white passes the ball, and ignore all the passes made by the team wearing black.

The funny part happens a short while into the experiment. Over the course of about ten seconds, somebody in a scraggly gorilla costume calmly walks into the middle of the weaving players, faces the camera, silently thumps their chest, and walks out of view.

Afterward, when test subjects are asked the final pass count, they almost always give the correct number or one that is very close. But when asked about the gorilla, only about half of them report seeing it! Researcher Daniel Memmert had people wear an eye tracker during his version of the experiment, and he found that the ones who missed the gorilla looked *right at it* for up to a full second—but it never registered in their minds!

Psychology professor Daniel Simons, another researcher on the "gorilla experiment," summarized the effect this way:

> The failure to notice people in gorilla suits is really a natural byproduct of something that we do quite well and that's very important to us, which is focusing our attention. We need to be able to filter out the distractions from our world and not let them interfere with our ability to do the task we're trying to do. . . . We only see those things that we focus our attention on."[20]

Gorillas and Goals

What's a guy in a gorilla suit got to do with getting qualified? Simply this: where you focus your attention can make or break your plans, both in life and on this journey.

When you focus on what's hard, bad, or wrong, your progress comes to a halt. Your attention is no longer on the work at hand, and you don't finish your task or resolve your problem. This is true whether the obstacle is real or imagined.

That's why you have to be the boss of your Reticular Activating System. At your instruction, it will keep you fixed on the goal—on what's beyond the barriers—not the barriers themselves. If you will train your brain to laser-focus on the two things that I'll explain below, your RAS will "bounce" the negative and the unnecessary from your brain, and you'll finish what you started.

1. Focus on the Positive.

What do you do when you hit an obstacle? Go to the positive. Now, I don't mean that you ignore the obstacle. I mean you look for the positive in it.

Do you remember the last time you paid for the person behind you in the restaurant drive-through? What happened next? Your generosity inspired the person behind you to be generous to the car after them, and so on.

This is a *thing*. Biologists call it a *positive feedback loop*, and we see this operating in nature when all the fruit on an apple tree begins ripening at the same time. It all begins thanks to one good apple. As that first apple ripens, it emits ethylene gas through its skin, and the nearby apples start "cooking with the same gas," so to speak. Almost overnight, the tree will be bursting with fruit that's ready for picking.[21]

When most people face an obstacle, what they see is a big, fat, hairy problem. But it's not really a big, fat, hairy problem—it's a golden opportunity. When you look for the positive in any setback, it allows your brain to start seeing the possibilities at play. The next time you're faced with something that feels negative, choose one good "starter thought"—something with a better spin on the situation. Your RAS can take that positivity and quickly ripen it into all kinds of great outcomes.

Let's play this out. Suppose you hurt yourself trimming bushes over the weekend, and you wind up in the emergency room with stitches and an antibiotic. You haven't met your medical deductible yet, so most of the money will have to come out of pocket, which means dipping into your emergency fund.

The obstacle is real—you're not denying it—but you're not giving it any gas either. Instead, you can empower a positive feedback loop by telling your RAS to look at the opportunity.

In the past, you may have thought, *My dream is doomed! This is the worst possible time for a financial hit!* But now that you've tapped in to your superpower, take this chance to reset your focus—and to redirect your dialogue along with it.

Begin with, *This actually could've been a lot worse.* That starter thought will then produce other positive thoughts, including brand-new ideas: *I can replace that money pretty fast. Come to think of it, I just need to find some side jobs to rebuild the emergency fund. And while I'm at it, I think I'll challenge myself to save up more than before—just because I can!*

You see how this works? You've essentially kick-started your brain to work for you. Soon, you'll start to see all kinds of possibilities crossing your path: the notice you've never glanced at before that somebody posted on the job board at work, some random magazine headline in the checkout line that sparks an idea, the ads or recommendations you suddenly see popping up on social media. Even as you're doing chores around the house, you'll come up with creative ways to earn additional money that you hadn't thought of.

Understanding the power of your focus and mastering your mind will be a game changer for you. I haven't given you the science just to prove what works. I want you to use the science to create momentum, build up your confidence, and *finish* getting qualified no matter what setbacks you encounter.

2. Focus on Finishing.

The second way you redirect your Reticular Activating System is to set your sights on the win, not the work in the moment. I ran the Rock 'n' Roll Half Marathon in Nashville a few years ago, and somewhere around mile six, I hit the wall. For those of you who don't run long distance, hitting the wall is what it sounds like: My legs cramped up and felt like I had knives stuck in them. I wasn't running anymore—I was hobbling along like a wounded wildebeest. I couldn't get relief from the cramping. In every way, my body was shouting, "I'm DONE!"

For the next few miles, I was just gutting it out. Those miles were nothing but sheer will—mind over matter. At this point in the race, as running coach Jes Woods describes it, "Your strength doesn't come from your body, it comes from your heart . . . and that fire in your belly asking you, 'How bad do you want it?'"[22]

And I wanted to reach that finish line badly. I'd promised myself I would, and I had family and friends cheering me on. But my body . . . it was running on fumes. So I had to switch my focus. Instead of listening to how I felt, I started focusing on how I would finish. And you know what? I found some new life because my focus was *past the wall*. I got a bit of a second wind. I began to pick up a little speed. And my exhilaration only grew as I closed in on the finish line.

Your focus propels you to the finish. As soon as you hit the wall and you're tempted to quit, that's the time for your brain to take charge. *Shift your thoughts from the present to the peak.* That's how you get through!

By ignoring your desire to quit and focusing only on the reward of finishing, you shut down all your complaints and concentrate on how awesome the mountaintop is going to be. I had to use my mind to see it, taste it, and feel it. I saw myself crossing the finish line, and it kept me going when I most wanted to quit.

Do that for yourself as you're getting qualified. Is your momentum slowing? Are you trudging? Imagine the moment when you hear: "You're hired!" Imagine getting up in the morning and spending your workday in your sweet spot. In your mind's eye, hold that first dream-job paycheck in your hand. How incredible is it to get paid for doing what you love?

Don't let the finish line out of your sights. Be so focused on the peak that no emotion or obstacle can stop you.

Do What You Have to Do

There's no way around it: getting qualified isn't sexy. Of the seven stages on the path to meaningful work, Stage 2 is the marathon. It's going to take a while. There are going to be seasons when you have to do things you don't want to. You're on course, doing the right thing—it's just not the fun thing.

In the movie *The Great Debaters*, a young man named Junior rushes into his dad's office and proudly announces to his father (played by Forest Whitaker) that he's just made the debate team. After a brief conversation, his father replies, "Extracurricular activities like the debate team are fine, but you must not take your eye off the ball, son."

"Yes, sir," Junior says.

"So, what do we do here?"

You can tell by the boy's face that he has heard his father make this statement a thousand times, and he says: "We do what we have to do so we can do what we want to do."

Dad then asks, "What do you have to do right now?"

"My homework," says the boy.

"So get to it."[23]

I'll let this dad's challenge be the challenge to all of us: Get to it. Stay the course even when it's hard or unpleasant. Use your mind to help you. Pay the price so you can have the prize.

Your entire journey may take three, five, seven, or twelve years. But the mountaintop moment awaits. Keep that in your sights.

Do what you have to do so that one day you can do what you want to do.

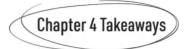

Remember This

What you focus on is what you act on.

You Got This

You are the only one who can stop you.

Do this

Focus on your finish line every day, and do what you
have to do so you can do what you want to do.

STAGE 3

Get Connected for Opportunities

5

You Already Know Everyone
You Need to Know

I'm pretty shy," admitted Amber, "so meeting strangers scares me. I never know what to say, and I stumble over my words. I just feel so embarrassed and awkward . . . I can't imagine ever being able to network and land my dream job."

Marcus told me, "Ken, the field I'm interested in is pretty specialized. I've never met anybody who works in it."

Shelly was clear on what she wanted to do but said, "I don't know people at that company, and even if I did, getting in there is ultracompetitive."

Then there was Brian: "I live in a small town. Not many options here."

People say it many different ways, but Stage 3—Get Connected almost always includes one massive hurdle in their minds: *I don't know enough people.*

With these next two chapters, we're going to blast that hurdle into tiny pieces. The truth is: *You* do *know enough people.* Period. What you need to do is think differently about the people you're already connected to.

Remember playing memory matching games when you were a child? You and your opponent turned over cards with different pictures on them, trying to memorize where the matches were. Getting connected to the person who will help you take the next step toward your dream job is similar to that game. As you connect with each person you know, you find out who they know and continue the connection process until you're talking to a decision-maker who can hire you. *The secret to getting connected is not just who* you *know, but all the people they know too.*

I'll give you an example. Brian is an accountant. He wants a side job helping local accounting firms through tax season, but nobody in his area has posted any openings. And though he lives in a small town, he doesn't know any other employees at those businesses. If I were to ask Brian to guess how many people he knows between friends, family, and acquaintances, he'd estimate around two hundred. That seems to be the average number that people quote me, even those who are from small towns.

If Brian knows two hundred people, then it's safe to say that each of the people he knows probably knows at least two hundred people, and maybe more. That amounts to a huge web of connections! He's linked to thousands of people already. And that's good news for all of us. No matter your limitations, you're three, maybe four, connections away from getting hired. All the people you need to get *the* job at *that* company are already there! Your job is to find them.

I can hear some of you now:

"But, Ken, I live on a tropical island." *Great! You know enough people.*

"But, Ken, I'm self-employed and have only three friends besides my dog." *You already have a connection to the person who will ultimately connect you to your dream job.*

"But, Ken, only twenty people in the entire galaxy are doing the work I'd love to do." *Perfect! Right now, you know all the people you need to know to get started.*

Just connect the dots you already have.

That's what Stage 3—Get Connected—is all about.

Make the Match

Once I started down the broadcasting path, I decided I wanted to try talk radio. I'd gotten some limited TV experience and had been hosting a leadership podcast out of Atlanta for a while, and that had given me an idea for my own radio show. I just needed to find a local station that would give me a chance.

Way easier said than done. In those days, podcasts were not a credible broadcast experience, and I was a no-name in a huge city full of famous names. Oh, and one more thing: I'd never met anyone in talk radio in Georgia.

To make up for all that, I planned to flood the market with phone calls to every station with a talk format. I was willing to cast my net wide for as long as it took, until somebody bit.

I must've cold-called five station managers. More than once. And I left messages. Multiple messages.

I received exactly zero callbacks.

Next round? I got *creative*. I sent emails.

You can guess the result . . . more radio silence. To those five station managers, I was a complete stranger. I'd have to find another way in. I needed a face-to-face somehow.

Since nothing else was working, I started from scratch. I made a list of everybody I knew (with paper and pencil, of course)—family, friends, and acquaintances—looking for a connection to someone in radio. I figured I had nothing to lose. Cold contacts had meant the cold shoulder everywhere I turned. At least with my list, I could follow up with people who would actually speak to me! It gave me another layer to explore. And as long as I had layers, I had some hope.

When I was done writing, my sheet of paper didn't just include the guys I played golf with and my buddies from high school. It also included people like the super friendly barista at the local coffee shop, the owner of the pizza place we loved, our neighbors, and a few people from the gym where I worked out.

Elizabeth was on that list too. She was a friend of a friend who'd needed some business advice about sponsorship sales for a nonprofit a few months earlier. I'd met with her as a favor to our mutual friend and given her an hour or so of time. I hadn't seen her since that day, but she qualified as an acquaintance so I wrote down her name.

As I did, a piece of our conversation came to mind. As we were talking that day, she'd made an offhand remark that she'd heard me on the leadership podcast and that her family owned a radio station in Atlanta. At that time, radio was not on my radar for the future, so I hadn't bothered to ask which station, but that one detail stuck.

Taking a deep breath, I picked up my phone, found Elizabeth's number, offered up a quick prayer for the right words to say, then I tapped the call button. As soon as Elizabeth heard my name, she said, "Ken! How are you?" Her warm response instantly made the call feel more like friends than business. I relaxed just a little. I was still anxious about how and when I should cut to the chase, but because she seemed unhurried and willing to chat, I decided to go with it.

Elizabeth excitedly updated me on how the nonprofit was doing and thanked me again for meeting with her. Then, people person that she is, she turned the conversation around: "Enough about me. Tell me how you're doing!"

Whew! The way she was treating me was helping to make this nerve-wracking conversation easier. She'd given me a natural opening to make my request. I took another deep breath. Time to put myself out there.

First, I shared about the career change I was making and my dream to do radio. I wanted her to hear some of my recent journey and my *why* versus "just the facts." And you know what? She really listened! I also confessed, "I've made lots of calls and sent emails to station managers, but I haven't heard anything back. I know you said your family owned a local radio station. Would you tell me more about the station, and, if you're open to it, would you get me a meeting with a decision-maker at the station?"

She did. Then she offered to connect me with her brother, who happened to be the CEO at the station in town.

In a matter of days, I was sitting in his office, pitching him my idea. It still seems pretty unreal to this day. Who knew that my tiny little act of meeting and helping a friend of a friend would open a door for me that had otherwise been dead-bolted shut. I'm so thankful to Elizabeth because her willingness to connect me with her brother is the *only* reason he agreed to meet with me.

I'm sure there were times during our interview when he wondered, *What planet did this guy come from?* But evidently he liked my idea enough to offer me a Saturday time slot, and version 1.0 of *The Ken Coleman Show* debuted a little later that year.

I kept turning over my relationship cards. Connected with an acquaintance from my list. And to my great relief and excitement, a job match was made.

The Strength of Weak Ties

I'll never be able to thank Elizabeth or her brother Jay enough. For her to do me such a huge favor, and for him to give me an interview when no one else would, was nothing but gracious.

That was one of my big takeaways from this experience. I knew relationships were important in my personal life, but I was experiencing firsthand how much they mattered in my career. *People make our work possible*—from career leaps and job changes to our day-to-day productivity.

What's interesting is that most people get hired not through close friends or family but through acquaintances—or "weak ties" as sociology professor Mark Granovetter calls them. They may be acquaintances of yours—folks you rarely see or have only met once or twice, like Elizabeth was for me. Or they could be someone who knows one or more of the people in your wider circle. Within one test group, almost

85 percent got hired through their acquaintances, not their everyday tribe.[24] Granovetter also discovered that more than 60 percent of these "informants," the acquaintances who told them about the job opening, got word of it through *their* weak ties.[25]

LinkedIn data confirms it. Only about one in eight new hires had a direct, "first-degree connection" to the company that hired them when they began their job search. So . . . eight out of every nine people who ultimately got the job didn't know anyone in the company themselves. Their remote, or indirect, connections—people two or three degrees removed from them—were their door openers.[26]

How are weak ties so helpful? They're "more likely to move in circles different from our own," reports Granovetter.[27] More ears and eyes in places you don't live, among people who haven't met each other, means more word of mouth about jobs you wouldn't hear of otherwise. And as everybody knows, word of mouth is the best advertising. People trust the referrals of people who know them.

Your connection doesn't have to be with an actual employee of a company, although that's ideal. A referral from a customer, a vendor, or a peer in the industry also carries weight with hiring managers and bosses. Their own personal connections matter too. These people have social circles, just like everyone else. Maybe the HR assistant at that company you've applied to was in a sorority with your neighbor's daughter. Or a manager at your dream company is friends with one of the dads from your kid's soccer team. These are great possibilities!

Just look at the data: *If you make it to the interview phase as a referral, you're twenty times more likely to be hired by a company than someone who only applied online.*[28] By comparison, less than 1 percent of those who apply to a typical job posting get hired without any connections.[29] That's about 250 to 1 odds.

Maybe you haven't met those outer-circle connections yet, but I'm going to show you how to do it. In this section, you'll learn how to find and reach these people, how to build strong connections naturally, and how to avoid the kinds of awkward conversations that we all associate with getting connected. We'll start by covering what connecting *isn't*.

What Connecting *Isn't*

What comes to mind when I say the words *Get Connected*? If you're like most people, the first thing you think of are dreadful networking events where you hand out business cards like Halloween candy and bounce between conversations like a ping-pong ball. But let me make one thing very clear: connecting *isn't* networking. I'm sure you've dealt with networkers. They're the brown-nosers. The users. The schmoozers. While talking with you, they scan the room like they have radar, looking for someone else more valuable than you. These people are value vampires—they suck the value out of you until they get what they need, and then they leave you for dead.

Many years ago I did business with a guy who was like that. "Clint" came on fast and strong—lots of compliments and smiles—making me feel valued. But with time, I began to feel like I wasn't important to him, except for what I could do for him. I could give you a long list of the things I noticed, but I'll shorthand it for you since you know the type.

Conversations with Clint were hollow. And as brief as he could make them. He didn't tell me anything of substance about himself or ask how things were really going in my world. He'd get on the phone: "Hey, how are ya? What's up, buddy?" And before I could answer, he'd be in full business mode: "That's good. Hey, man, quick question for ya." He was all about the result. For him. It was never the other way around.

As I spent time with him, I noticed he treated others the same way. Flattery and promises up front, but then he disappeared as soon as they delivered what he needed. He'd tell everybody, "Call me anytime," but there was never follow-through. You couldn't even guarantee he'd listen to your voice mails.

As you'd suspect, he left a lot of collateral damage. There were burned bridges everywhere. What really bugged me, though, was how you were sometimes guilty by association if you had worked with him. People trusted *you* a little less, wondering if you did business like he did.

I'm still cordial with Clint today, but I keep him at a distance. By the knowing glances around the table when his name comes up in certain circles, I'm guessing I'm not the only one.

This is one of the biggest problems with networking: it never leads to genuine relationships. It's too much like speed dating, where everyone is out for themselves and the sincere ones walk away feeling like a piece of meat.

The Difference between Connecting and Networking

What is it about networking that makes us feel uncomfortable? For one, networking is *intimidating*. It creates fear. You come into the conversations feeling "less than," in a sense, because you don't have the job, the expertise, or the connection that the person you're talking to has. Even extroverts find it hard to ask for something when they have nothing to offer in return. Nobody likes being in need.

Connecting, unlike networking, adjusts the balance because it gives you an eye toward the future. You may have only a sincere thank-you to offer the person today, but tomorrow is a different story! And you intend to be in their life long enough to help them out if the shoe's ever on the other foot.

Also, networking feels gross because it's *transactional.* It cheapens conversations—and people. To the networker, you're a name to drop or a rung on the industry ladder, not a person. What "transactors" don't realize is that they can only make so many transactions before the well runs dry. After a while, there won't be any more people to do business with.

Third, networking feels awful because it's *draining.* More often than not, the networker is a taker who gives nothing back—often, not even a thank-you. They get what they want from you and move on, circling back only when they need something else.

By comparison, connecting means you're both essentially making deposits into a joint account that you can each draw from. There's a spirit of humility and exchange that makes you want to return the favor, not just enjoy it. You're thinking long term about how you can give back and pay forward what they've done for you. It's not just about you, and it's not just about this moment in time.

So if you want a simple solution to all your networking problems and the icky feelings that come with them, don't network. Connect! Connecting is relational. It focuses on the whole person, the big picture versus the bottom line. Connecting with others is about investing in every interaction. You're asking questions and paying attention to how they respond. The other person feels listened to, valued, and in turn, they value you. You aren't viewing anyone through the lens of "What's in it for me?" and you aren't favoring one person over another due to their job title or place in the pecking order. When you seek relationships, nobody feels used.

Getting connected is a way of living. It's a lifelong habit of building authentic relationships. No matter where you are on your journey toward meaningful work, you can start doing this today. If you're just getting clear, start investing in people. If you're in debt and your dream job is on hold while you dig your way out, start investing in people. If you're still not convinced this path will even work, start investing in people.

People matter more than your position. They're the priority. Understanding this will make you successful personally and professionally. Make people your emphasis over getting any job, and then watch how that good will come back to you.

History's bestselling book promises us that it does. It says we reap what we sow. Sometimes people only view that in the negative sense, like, "Uh-oh, I'll get the cosmic smackdown if I don't do right by people." But if you check out that passage in the Bible, it doesn't end on the negative. After we're reminded that those who sow "sparingly will also reap sparingly," we're promised, "whoever sows bountifully will also reap bountifully."[30] In our professional journey, just like in all of our relationships, generosity and kindness are timeless. As you're on the path to meaningful work, remember to make relationship building part of your lifestyle. The good you put out into the world will boomerang back at you.

The Currency of Progress

Dabo Swinney was about as unlikely a hire as you could get. He had little of the typical experience you'd expect for a head coach of a top ACC football program. "The bottom line is when I hired him, he really didn't have credentials," said former Clemson athletic director Terry Don Phillips.[31]

So why did Terry Don hire Dabo? Ultimately, it was because of how Dabo treated people.

> "I just kept hearing about this energetic receivers coach we had and found myself wandering over to his side of the field," Phillips said. "I liked the way he coached his players, how he was tough on them, but was always teaching them and always there for them outside of football. It's not a facade with Dabo. He genuinely cares, and his players sense that."
>
> [Phillips] noticed how the players were always milling around Swinney's office when they weren't on the practice field or in class.
>
> "And not just receivers, but players from all positions," Phillips said. "Kids migrated to this particular coach, and that caught my eye."[32]

This is the power of valuing people and relationships. Yes, Dabo had the skills to do the job, but what got him hired was how he truly cared about the people he was working with. The players and other coaches weren't a means to a win or a title. He genuinely cared about them, and it was obvious to everyone.

Here's what I want you to see: *relationships are actually the currency of progress.* Think about it—the world revolves around currency. Money is what allows people to get what they want, go where they want, and live how they want. Relationships give us those opportunities in our work. Your relationships and connections are the bridge to the job you've been dreaming of and working toward. So make them a priority, always looking for ways to help others. You never know when the "blessing boomerang" will head back your way. If you're genuinely investing in others, you will see compound growth in your career.

A Small-but-Mighty Principle

Okay, let's recap. We've talked about the fact that you already know everyone you need to know to make the next step in your journey. We've also discussed that traditional networking is the wrong strategy— that the key to getting connected is building authentic relationships. So how does all of that work together to get you to your dream job? By a small-but-mighty principle I call the Proximity Principle. *Proximity* means getting near or being close to something. Applied to the process of getting connected, its operating principle is this:

> *In order to do what you want to do, you have to be around the people who are doing it and in the places it's happening. Then opportunity will find you.*

The "right people" are those who are doing what you would love to do, and the "right places" are where your ideal work is being done. As your talent and passion intersect with people who are already where you want to be, you get more opportunities, and through those opportunities, you meet more people. That's the Proximity Principle in action. Connect with the right people in the right places, and opportunity will find you.

This little principle is so powerful and effective that I've written an entire book about it by the same name. That book covers a lot of ground about who to build connections with and where to build them. I'll give you a brief summary in the next chapter, but you can check out *The Proximity Principle* to learn more. Once you know the *who* and the *where* of building connections, the only other piece is the *how*. We'll look at that in detail in chapter 6.

And for all of you introverts who are getting queasy at the thought of connecting like this—you're going to be surprised at how equipped you already are for making connections. So don't check out now. As for my fellow extroverts, you'll get some ideas that will help opportunity come to you even faster. Let's get to it!

Remember This

Most people get hired through acquaintances,
not family or close friends.

You Got This

Getting connected is not just about who you
know but all the people they know.

Do This

Make a list of all of your acquaintances—
people you know but are not close to.

6

The Art of Connecting

Kristen was frustrated. The day she called the show, she confessed, "I've sent out fifty resumés in five days and haven't received one response!" When I pressed her for a little more information, I found out that she had no personal connection in any of the companies she'd sent resumés to. To her knowledge, not a single friend, acquaintance, or friend of a friend was employed at any of the places she was targeting in her job search. She was feeling hopeless about her efforts and beginning to question herself.

Maybe you're feeling the same way. You've been out of the work-force and lost touch with the people you once knew. Or you're switching industries and haven't begun to connect with anyone in this new arena. The silver lining in times like these is that the lack of response has nothing to do with you personally. In Kristen's case, her resumé was simply stuck in a gigantic pile with hundreds of other unread resumés. When I was cold-calling producers back in Georgia, my voice mails and emails were also sitting unheard and unopened at radio stations across Atlanta. That approach just doesn't work.

What's needed is a change in strategy.

Where to Begin

Jake wanted to talk about getting connected in both a new place and a new career.

For eighteen years, he'd been working as a licensed electrician, but it wasn't his sweet spot. His sweet spot—inspired by growing up in an Air Force family—was to be a flight instructor. He thought he might even enjoy using his trade skills to work on the flight line with the aircraft directly.

Beyond the career switch, Jake was also planning to move from Virginia to Texas, where he knew no one besides family. In preparation for these changes, he'd spent the past six months sending out resumés with no luck.

Where does someone like him begin to get connected? This is where the Proximity Principle comes in. Rather than hoping for some luck to come his way, he can start by asking himself: *Who do I need to be around, and where do I need to be, so I can do what I love for a living?*

Several degrees of separation may be standing in your way as you ask yourself this same question. That's to be expected. But practicing the Proximity Principle will give you many ways to span the gap.

You never know what a couple of conversations over coffee might do. Or the difference that asking for a little help can make. One thing is for sure: by getting around the right people, you get invited to the right places where the path to your dream can begin. Like I said earlier, I go into a lot of detail about how to do this in my book *The Proximity Principle*, but I'll give you a brief overview here.

Who to Build Connections With: The Right People

Who do you need to know so that opportunity will find you? You're looking to create a web of connections between who you know and who you want to know.

The "right people," according to this principle, are the ones who can help you make the climb up the mountain. Be on the lookout for these five types of individuals:

1. *The Professors* instruct you on the skills you'll need to succeed in the field you want to work in. Their role is to help you gain relevant knowledge and connections for opportunities to get started in your desired field.

2. *The Producers* are winning in the field you want to be in, and they're accessible because they're owners or executives who create jobs, hire, and build teams. As these go-getters are generating opportunities, they'll willingly share their knowledge and offer direction. They're also great connectors themselves and can introduce you to more of the right people—and may eventually hire you.

3. *The Peers* accompany you on your journey. They're in the same stage of life as you, they share your values and your drive, and they'll encourage and challenge you when you need it.

4. *The Professionals* are the best of the best in their field. They are well-known and someone you look up to for their accomplishments and inspiration. While they may be very hard to meet in person, you can learn from them from afar.
5. *The Mentors* are the wise sages who offer guidance and accountability. These are accomplished, understanding people who are committed to guiding you on your journey.

Who are these five types of people on *your* path? Who can help move you farther along? Don't be afraid to ask them for help. You may get a few nos before you get a yes. Press on, though, because having these people on your side will make you unstoppable.

Where to Connect: The Right Places

Where do you need to be? The Proximity Principle states that, to get to your dream job, you need to be around the people who are doing your kind of work, in the places where that work is being done. Here are five places where opportunity can most easily find you:

1. *The Place Where You Are.* You don't have to make a cross-country move to find work you're passionate about. Everything you need to begin connecting is in your own zip code.

   For Jake, the future flight instructor, it's time to stop sending resumés and start showing up at airfields. He needs to become an "airport bum" whenever he clocks out of his day job. Nothing is stopping him from working part time or volunteering at a local airfield or airport. He can sweep floors, take out the trash, wash and fuel the planes—whatever they'll let him do. Once the people around him can see that he has the chops, and they know how hungry and humble he is, Jake may not even have to submit a resumé. But if he does, he'll be handing it to people who already know him.

2. *A Place to Learn.* This is where you'll get the licensing, certifications, or knowledge you'll need to be successful at the job you want to do. Check out the Education Question in chapter 3 for a great list of places to learn. And if you've been out of the workforce for at least two years, look for places that offer a "returnship" program. More and more companies are providing these short-term opportunities for people to refresh their skills while the organization considers them for a long-term fit.

3. *A Place to Practice.* This could look like volunteering, interning, or freelancing. Expect to do some or all of the work here for free, but you'll have room to turn your knowledge into experience. That's what counts. Meanwhile, you'll benefit from the feedback, the freedom to fail, and the confidence you get from the chance to practice.

4. *A Place to Perform.* This is where you actually get in the door and start making money for doing your thing. It could be an entry-level position or somewhere higher up the ladder. As long as it's in the field you want, with people who are doing what you want to do, you'll be making connections *and* making sure this is the right career choice for you.

5. *A Place to Grow.* These are the jobs that will maximize your strengths and offer clear opportunities for growth. Sometimes

finding a place to grow means broadening your search and relocating. Whether or not you need to move, this is where you're within reach of your dream.

Jason is a former tech at Apple retail whose dream job is to serve as an on-site tech at any of the Disney parks. His challenge is finding a way in, since the Disney career page is showing no tech listings anywhere in North America.

Fortunately, the company website isn't the only place for him to look. He may be able to find other points of access among his acquaintances. For example, Jason could check with his former retail managers and coworkers to see if they know of anyone at Disney or one of its partner companies. Entering through the back door, by way of a partner company, is just as legit as applying directly to Disney.

In all of these ways, Jason would be putting himself in the right place to make connections. So can you. You just have to think outside the box.

How to Connect

Once you know who you want to connect with and where, you're ready to step out and seize your opportunities. As you watch, listen, learn, and connect with people in those environments, you'll meet more of the right people, and as a result, you'll get into more of the right places. And each connection will put you one step closer to your dream job.

Here's what you need to do to get a quick start using the power of proximity so you can make progress. Take it step by step.

1. *Make a list of the people you know.* Like I said in chapter 5: you know more people than you think. When I made my list, hoping to find some radio connections in Atlanta, it was longer than I expected, simply because I gave myself permission to look beyond the usual connections. You'll find the same to be true for you.

Start with the obvious—your closest, everyday circles of family and favorite friends—and then work outward. Don't forget about these middle-ring folks that I know you know:

- Coworkers and executives from previous workplaces
- People in your professional groups and associations
- Social media connections (especially those on LinkedIn)
- People in your phone contact list
- Community connections such as your family physician and kids' teachers
- People in your social clubs or fellow hobbyists
- Fellow church members
- Former classmates

Who do they know, or what places do they have access to, that they could connect you with?

2. *Inform the people you know about what you want to do.* Tell your inner circle (family members, close friends) first: "I want to get *there*. I want to do *this*." But don't stop with them. Really focus on your remotest, outer-circle acquaintances as you're seeking leads. These are people you're friendly with but don't know beyond a certain setting— like your mail carrier, the clerk at the grocery who calls you by name, your favorite waiter or waitress at the local restaurant, the parents of other players on your kid's soccer team or in the marching band. They all have their own connections, and among their circles may be the connection you're looking for.

3. *Ask for help.* The most important question people never ask is, "Will you help me?"

We don't ask for two primary reasons: fear of rejection and pride—no one wants to appear helpless. You have to knock on some doors if you truly want people to help you. It's rare that someone will come up to you, out of the blue, and ask, "What can I do for you?" So set aside your pride and silence your fear long enough to try.

I know, I know. This can feel big-time uncomfortable. Even for an extrovert like me, I've worried that I'd be bothering people. That could happen, but it won't happen much if you ask with these tips in mind:

- You're only asking them one time. You're not going to keep coming back with, "Who else do you know?"
- You're asking *about* something, not *for* something. It's information instead of action. With this approach, you can put aside the fear of rejection because you're only asking for a connection. Your point person won't have to do any heavy lifting. You'll do the work.

  Some people will want to introduce you to their connections themselves; others will give you contact info and say, "Tell them I sent you." But almost nobody will feel put out by hearing you out and handing over an email address or a phone number—especially if you've had conversations with them before.

- People are people. We've all been helped by someone else along the way and we want to add value to the world. Most people will feel valuable when you ask for their help and will help when approached the right way.

Scott Swedberg, founder and CEO of The Job Sauce and a former hiring manager with LinkedIn, has some real encouragement about asking for help: "My connections will happily introduce me to their connections if they like me, know the connection, and are confident in my skills."[33]

So, the next time you're at your daughter's game or watching your son's practice, start getting to know those other parents. (Remember: this is a lifelong habit of caring about other people and building relationships with them!) Ask them questions about themselves. Show some interest in them first. The very nature of caring for others is that (usually) they will be inclined to help you when your time comes.

In that "ask" conversation, you can say something as simple as, "I'm looking to do this. Do you know anybody in that space? Anybody who works at that company?" As long as you've been nice to these people—and I know you have been!—they aren't going to consider you a nuisance. They'll want to help you because of who you are.

4. Create a connection to-do list. The next step to connecting is to create a to-do list. Once you have some names and companies, do some research to learn more. You're not only deciding which connections make sense for you but which ones to start with. How many degrees away from the hiring manager are they? The goal is to get as close as possible to the decision-maker.

This is also the time for you to plan how you will approach each of those people or companies. What will you say to those you're calling? How will your introductory email read? Spend time preparing so you're not having to think on your feet.

Now hear me out. When I say "research," I'm not suggesting online stalking. Don't dig in like this is a background check. Being a creeper won't get you anywhere! Your goal is to gather *public* information that you can use to make a deeper connection in real life. If you're meeting with a friend of a friend, have your friend tell you a few "need to knows" about the person.

You're listening and looking for commonalities with those individuals. Scott Swedberg suggests that you're more likely to get help from indirect connections who you have some sort of shared bond with. For example, if you're both alumni from the same college or are from the same part of the world, have a mutual interest or hobby, or have kids who are the same age, you can always use those common bonds to break the ice and ease the way with strangers.[34]

I was shocked when I gained a mentor using this approach.

Bob Rathbun was the play-by-play announcer for the Atlanta Hawks and the Atlanta Braves. He'd also been the sportscaster on one of our local TV stations in my hometown when I was in high school, so in a sense, I'd grown up with him. After Stacy and I moved to Atlanta, I turned on a Braves game one day—and there was that dynamic, familiar voice, doing the play-by-play. Since Bob was in broadcasting and I was considering moving into sports broadcasting at the time, I decided to reach out to him. Why not? We had a hometown connection, and the worst that could happen was that he might ignore me. *Wouldn't be the first time.*

I first called the Braves office to get his contact info. Then I sent him a heartfelt email. I mentioned growing up in Virginia and watching him on WTKR News Channel 3 and talked about how much I appreciated his career and how happy I'd been to hear his voice doing Atlanta sports. I also mentioned that I recently moved to the area and was working for leadership expert John Maxwell's organization and that I'd like to express my appreciation to him in person someday if I could.

Imagine my surprise when he replied the next day: "Thanks for the kind words and for reaching out to me. I'd love to get together sometime. Incidentally, I'm a huge fan of John Maxwell's work. Would you be able to introduce me to John?"

I was so pumped to hear from him! I was also honored to be able to do a favor for someone that I looked up to. I sent Bob tickets to a local event of John's, plus a green-room pass, and introduced Bob to John so they could spend some time together.

That was the beginning of a friendship that continues to this day. Bob never connected me for a job, but he has taught me, encouraged me, and become a mentor throughout my journey. The lesson? Reaching out is always worth the risk of rejection.

5. Reach out, make the connections, and set up some meetings. Extroverts are usually ready to roll at this point. But I caution everyone to use social media thoughtfully throughout this process. LinkedIn is great for information but not for connection. The other sites—Facebook, Instagram, and so on—aren't good ways to message people either, unless you've been told that's how the person wants to connect. The traditional forms of contact are still the best: emails, phone calls, in-person meetings.

Introverts, take a deep breath. You can do this. In fact, you're naturally better at this than extroverts. This is about a one-to-one connection. You don't need to chat up a room full of people here or contact everyone in the same day. You can go at your own pace. Keep it in perspective: you're looking to get a little time for genuine conversation, one person at a time. Try some of these ideas to take away some of the intimidation factor:

- Ask for fifteen minutes of your connection's time at their workplace, and tell them you'll bring doughnuts or bagels. Or depending on how well you know them, you might ask for a brief office tour and lunch afterward—on you.
- Offer to treat them to coffee or lunch, and suggest a time limit on the front end. Knowing it's only a thirty- or forty-five-minute commitment, for example, makes it less pressured for both of you.
- Volunteer in the line of work that interests you. Even a few hours of strong, hands-on help from you can leave a lasting impression on valuable connections.
- And for those connections that you seem to click with, you can ask about the possibility of job-shadowing them for part of a day. It's a great way to test-drive your dream.

Carrie was in an interesting situation that I'm sure some of you can relate to. She had vast experience as a supply-chain director and applied for her dream job at her dream company. She even discovered an in-house connection after she applied: a former student of hers. The problem was, the company put the position on hold before Carrie ever got to meet with anybody in human resources. She wanted to know: "How do I keep this possibility alive without being pushy?"

Her sense is correct: it would send the wrong message were she to ask for a meeting with a hiring manager herself. But if her in-house connection was willing to make the request, that would be a different story. The employee could go to human resources and say, "I realize this position is on hold, but I know one of the applicants, Carrie, and she's really great. She also has a ton of experience. Could I bring her in to meet with you for just five minutes? Just so you can have a face with the name?"

Again, no one is being put out here. It's a couple of minutes in anyone's day. If the hiring manager says no or Carrie's connection isn't comfortable making the request, Carrie can always seek other possibilities while she waits. But if everyone is willing? Then her resumé goes straight to the top of the pile when the company is ready to hire!

As you're finding ways to connect with new people, I want you to keep in mind one very important thing: *with strangers or connections you barely know, it's extra important to respect their time.* So request a specific number of minutes up front—*minutes*, not hours—and honor whatever the connection agrees to. This earns their trust. It also leaves a big impression since so few people do it.

I know people who have gone so far as to set the alarm on their phone before starting the meeting. That way they make sure to keep to the clock. The fact that you care so much about someone else's time speaks volumes. It may also persuade them to stay longer and keep talking. But do so only at their request!

How to Connect Like an Introvert

Now that we've covered the who, where, and how of connecting, we need to look at the best ways to make those connections meaningful. Ironically, the people who are best at authentically connecting with others are often the introverts who think they aren't very good at it. Introverts don't tend to be big talkers, and they usually feel uncomfortable with self-promotion. The thought of a cocktail party fills them with dread. But they excel at the art of connecting whether they realize it or not.

Sonya was surprised to learn what a strength being able to connect authentically can be. She is a strong introvert who, through the recommendations of a couple of her connections, was recruited for her dream job at a small start-up. The company had narrowed down their choices to her and another candidate, and they flew both of them in for a day of interviews. The main interviewer, Joey, would be the supervisor of that position.

Sonya had never met anyone at the company, so she felt pretty nervous as her flight landed. But she was also excited about the prospects for this job.

While Joey's warmth and friendliness helped put her at ease right away, what threw Sonya off was his interview style. For the entire day, he shared stories about himself and their industry and the work being done at this start-up company. During their seven hours together, he asked only three or four questions based on her resumé. Mostly, she engaged by commenting on his stories and asking him follow-up questions.

She had prepared a couple of job-related questions, and she did find a way to ask those. Otherwise, it was about as opposite of an interview as you could imagine. The introvert in her was relieved, since she didn't like talking about herself anyway. But professionally, she was upset with herself. She worried that she'd had almost no opportunity to share what she might contribute to the company's efforts.

Recapping the day when she got home that evening, Sonya disappointedly told her roommate, "I think I just listened myself out of the job."

She was even more convinced of it as one week went by, then two, then three—with no word back from the company. *Why else would they take so long?* But when Joey called her, he explained the administrative holdup they'd had. Sonya hadn't blown it after all. The job was hers.

Not long after she started at the company, Joey told her, "One of the reasons I chose you was because of how well you listened. I figured that if you were that good at listening to me and all my rabbit trails, you would listen well to our clients, and that is something they need."

To all you introverts out there, you often don't realize it, but you shine when you're connecting! These one-on-one situations are when you're at your best: Being sincere. Asking good questions. Listening closely. Really paying attention to whoever you're talking to. Whether you're naturally introverted or extroverted, we would all do well to connect like an introvert. No matter your personality, let's look at five specific ways to make your connections count.

Best Practices for Connecting

So what do great connectors do right? These five things:

1. They are present and think long term.
2. They add value by serving.

109

3. They focus on learning instead of advancing.
4. They watch the clock.
5. They follow up like a pro.

We'll look at each one in more detail.

1. Be present and think long term. Understand that conversations and contact info are only the beginning. No one needs to work the room, pass out five hundred business cards, or fake their way through an interview ever again. The person who gets hired is the one who hands out five cards to the right five people, and then follows up with them later in meaningful ways. Connecting means building toward a relationship with the intent of many future conversations. It's all about building a connection for the long haul.

One of the benefits of doing this is that it keeps you grounded during the entire process of getting connected. When you're thinking about building long-term relationships, you see people differently and hear conversations differently. You remember the details better—their kids' names, the surgery their spouse just went through, the book they just read . . . or, like in my case, that their family owns a radio station. You're concerned more with meaningful conversation and common bonds, and less about yourself, job titles, or getting off the phone as quickly as possible.

Another benefit to long-term thinking is that it helps you combat the nerves that have a way of showing up for important connections. You know what I'm talking about. You're just about to dive into the conversation but you start to feel really nervous and forget what you want to say. Like when a guy is interested in a girl but thinks she's out of his league and he turns into a driveling dufus. Why does this happen? *Because he's focusing on himself, not on her.* The same is true for you. If you'll focus more on the other person, listening carefully to the details they're sharing, your nerves will calm and you'll be able to better navigate the anxiety you're experiencing. And *this* will lead to a good connection.

2. *Add value by serving.* Look for ways to serve and add value to the other person. You're not just connecting for you. Think of how you can benefit them or their organization, and then practice how to communicate not only your idea for service but also your heart behind it.

When I first approached the leaders at Catalyst, a Christian leadership event, about starting a podcast for them, I didn't open with what a great opportunity it was for me. I was thinking about how it could help them. I talked them through what podcasting was (it was very new at that point!), how starting one had very little risk for them, and how it had the potential to actually help Catalyst reach their goals. I would create the show and host it for free in exchange for the experience and the ability to use their platform. Because a few of the guys knew and trusted me, they said yes.

Looking for ways to help another person feels very different than asking for a handout or a huge favor. When you have a mindset of service, you connect and communicate far more powerfully.

3. *Focus on learning, not advancing.* Instead of approaching a connection by telling them what you want to do and where you want to go, tell them what you want to learn and who you want to become.

Arrogance is seriously unattractive. Your connections don't need to hear about how great you are. It's better for them to *see* who you are. They will naturally pick up a lot about you from what you say, like the kinds of questions you ask and how you speak about and to other people. Your goal isn't to impress them. Your goal is to be curious and learn something.

I know of many introverts who have trained themselves to prepare a few questions, and then they go into a conversation genuinely wanting to learn about who they're talking to and what this person does. Rather than worrying about their own goals, they focus on their connection as a source of knowledge and wisdom and see where that leads. Do as they do. Listen twice as much as you talk, and treat your connection's time and input as being more important than your own. Because it is.

Besides mentioning a shared bond or two from your research and a little talk of the person who connected you, some good questions to ask are:

- How did you get your job?
- What drew you to it?
- Tell me about the path you took. How much of it was education versus learning on the job?
- What advice do you have for someone like me who's interested in landing a job like yours?
- Would you tell me which skills and traits you think make you most successful in your role?
- What are your favorite things about your work? Which parts aren't your favorite?
- What are you working on right now that really excites you?
- Is there anyone else you would recommend that I talk to?

Notice that I've changed up the wording. This is more natural and should help the conversation flow. Also, be sure to ask follow-up questions as they come to you. Write them down in the moment if you need to so you can remember them. And lastly, take good notes. Don't assume you're going to remember everything they said.

Sometimes a person will ask what *you* bring to the table (it *is* a connection for work purposes after all). So it's important that you're able to articulate an answer. This is where your purpose statement can help. Go back to the work you did in chapter 2 and on the Get Clear Career Assessment (which you can find at ramseysolutions.com/get-clear). Review those a few times before your conversation. If you're on the phone, have a copy of it in front of you. Practice sharing it naturally, explaining not only your talent but your passion for what you're wanting to do. People also love to know the story behind your dream (the brief version!), so be prepared to share your *why*.

As you're talking with your connections, remember that people don't remember someone who spent a few minutes giving them an elevator pitch. They will, however, remember someone who took the time to get to know them and share their heart.[35] Almost everybody enjoys talking about themselves as long as they know that the asker cares to hear them out.

4. Watch the clock. We've talked about the fact that people like it when you honor their time. It's just one way to show how much you value them. It also shows them how intentional you are to maximize your time with them. While there will be a bit of small talk at the beginning, it's okay for you to turn the discussion deeper when you sense the time is right. You can even tell the person: "I know your time is limited. Do you mind if I ask you a couple of questions?"

Take this approach, and it won't matter whether you're talking to an extrovert or an introvert. The extrovert will be glad to have the chance to talk. The introvert will be relieved to have something of substance to talk about. It's a win-win for everybody. You're going to make a good impression. And your authentic interest makes people far more likely to want to help you.

5. _Follow up like a pro._ That means be grateful before, during, and after you connect. Tone matters—be "classy" grateful, not "flattery" grateful. Don't weird them out by going overboard.

Within twenty-four hours of your meeting, send a thank-you email or handwritten note for your new connection's time and advice. Mention something specific that stood out to you from the conversation. And express your enthusiasm for the things you learned. You can also show your gratitude by complimenting them online or to the person who connected you. Undoubtedly, your compliments to that mutual friend will get back to the person you met with.

Check back in with them on a relational level every so often. That means just to say hi, without expecting anything in return. It can go a long way if, after a few months, you reconnect simply to say another brief thank-you and to update the person on your status, but without asking them for anything further.

Connection Is Your Contribution

Connecting with others is about so much more than getting your dream job. Make sure you're passing the value of connections along to others even as you're on your climb. It's part of your contribution as a person—who you've helped, who you've encouraged, who you've invested in.

Seek to bless others. Giving of yourself is part of your legacy as a human being. When you follow the Ramsey Baby Steps, you start giving 10 percent of your income away on the day you begin, even if you have debt. It's the same with giving of yourself. No matter what stage you're in on the path to meaningful work, you can start connecting with and investing in others *today*. This is paying it forward. And in return, you will be blessed. If you give as a habit, when you are in need, you'll never want for anything. Develop deep, long-lasting, thoughtful connections and it will do more than help you get your dream job. It will enrich your life in countless ways.

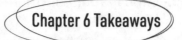

Remember This

When you're around the right people and in the
right places, opportunities find you.

You Got This

People *want* to help you, and they *will* help you.

Do This

Review and identify the people and places you need
to be around and in. Then start connecting.

STAGE 4

Get Started on the Journey

7

The Enemies of Progress

After getting clear, getting qualified, and getting connected, you're finally ready to get started. This is a big moment because it marks the beginning of the actual climb to your professional peak—your dream job!

What do I mean by that? Well, you don't just decide to climb Mount Everest one day, step out your front door, and start climbing. You make the decision to climb the mountain and then begin lengthy preparations in order to succeed. That's what Stages 1–3 are all about—the preparation. You've researched and purchased your climbing equipment. You've trained physically and mentally. You've flown to the other side of the world and then spent several days or weeks getting to base camp.

Now—today—you're at South Base Camp in Nepal, 17,600 feet above sea level. The preparations are finished. You open the flap of your tent in your cold-weather gear, step out onto the rocky soil, and see the snow-covered giant of a mountain looming in front of you. Your body feels electric. Tomorrow morning you start the trek up the mountain, and you're feeling excited, nervous, and a little tired already. Can you see yourself there?

Well, friends, welcome to Stage 4. This is Getting Started. You're at base camp today on the path to meaningful work. But if you're anything like me, as you stare up at the mountain in front of you, it actually looks a lot more treacherous than you thought it would—and you may be starting to second-guess yourself.

I'm not sure I'm ready . . . Should I have trained longer?

What if I fail?

Is this mission worth everything I have done and will encounter?

The stakes get considerably higher from this point forward on your path. There's not a lot of risk sitting on your couch researching ice axes and glove liners on your laptop! But now, your life is on the line. And when you're talking about work, it's your dream that's at stake—and potentially your family's livelihood. So if you're feeling hesitant at this point, that's actually a good sign. It means you understand the gravity of what you're about to start.

Ironically, Stage 4 is exciting and sad. So many people will do the work in Stages 1–3 . . . *but then never actually start the climb.* They'll get clear about their dream, they'll get qualified and connected, but they won't ever seize opportunities and leave base camp. Why? Because there are forces at play whose sole mission is to stop you from climbing (and really, stop your progress no matter where you are on the journey). So in chapter 7 we're going to take a close look at those forces and equip you to combat, counteract, and overcome everything and everyone standing in your way. Because, friends, the world needs what you have to offer and it's go time!

The Enemies

Everywhere he turned, Rob felt cornered. *I've been preparing for this for three years*, he thought. *I can't turn back now, but I'm not sure if I should move forward either. I'm stuck!*

This wasn't just frustration talking. He could no longer see his future clearly, and it worried him.

He did have a dream, though. One that drove him to pay off debt, learn new skills for a new field, and sacrifice to save money for the career transition. He was a high school teacher, but after being in the classroom for nine years, he realized he wanted to create a community mentoring program that connected high school students to successful professionals. He also loved real estate and realized that becoming a successful real estate agent could produce the income and freedom he needed to launch his mentoring program.

Anytime he thought of *that*, Rob's spirits lifted. But then he'd remember he hadn't sold a house yet and didn't have any clients, and the pit in his stomach would return.

"This is why I feel trapped," Rob admitted to me. "I know I really need to leave my teaching job to take this next step, but even though I've saved up three months of my salary, I don't know how long it will take me to sell enough houses to provide for my family."

The money. That's what really took the wind out of him. Though Rob and his wife had a good plan, every time he thought about starting out on the journey, it felt like a punch in the gut. His vision for the future was blurring by the day. *Maybe now isn't the right time to go for the dream*, he worried.

No matter how clear you've gotten, you'll have moments in these later stages where you start to lose heart or lose focus. Sometimes this will be due to actual barriers in your way. Other times, you'll find your-self being confronted by an opponent you weren't planning on. He'll look like Goliath, and he will take your focus off your path. As you enter Stage 4 and start your climb, you must be aware of the enemies of progress so you recognize them when they show up. Notice I didn't say "if" they show up, because I can assure you—they will.

Meet the Villains

I'm ashamed to admit that I watched a lot of professional wrestling when I was growing up. It was bad story lines and bad acting and bad guys—just bad television. And I couldn't stop watching it. The best drama happened before the match. It was all about the pre-match locker room interview, the entrance, and the buildup to the match. The wres-tlers would parade into the interview with an entourage, wearing masks and capes, drenched in sweat, with menacing faces and muscles flexed. Sometime before their exit, you just knew at least one of these guys was going to grab the mic and start yelling threats at his opponent, maybe even smashing a couple of chairs for emphasis. It was all part of the show.

None of it was real. It was entertainment designed to attract the attention of the audience, and it was predictable. These loudmouths came back to fight every week at the same time.

It's not that different when the enemies of our progress—Fear, Doubt, and Pride—dramatically strut into our day. Just like the fake wrestlers throwing tantrums in tights, promising doom and destruction, causing drama every time they show up. That's just what they do.

Now imagine if I could take you behind the scenes in one of those eye-opening documentaries that exposes the tricks of their trade. You'd see that Fear, Doubt, and Pride are liars who specialize in smoke and mirrors. They rely on confusion and illusion to hold you back.

Were you the kid who feared getting the shot at the doctor's? In reality, it was a pin prick that lasted a split-second, right? But your fear convinced you it was going to feel like they stabbed you with a spear. Fear, Doubt, and Pride are masters at magnifying our emotions to the extreme. That's one of their trademarks. They push us past common sense until we're locked up from looking at our worst-case scenario. The odds of utter ruin and complete disaster are about a zillion to one. But their tactics can take the fight right out of us, causing us to turn and run back to the locker room of life.

Understand the Playbook of the Enemy

When Fear, Doubt, and Pride are shouting at us, our brains can instantly flip to survival mode—the fight, flight, or freeze response that we see in spooked animals. It's sometimes called *lizard brain*. For about ninety seconds, it causes us to become a one-eyed zombie with a hyper-focus that blocks out everything but the threat.

This protective response is a blessing when the threat is real. The problem is, with so many unknowns as we're getting started, lizard brain sometimes perceives *everything* as a threat. It will automatically assume everything that Fear, Doubt, or Pride is shouting is legit. Then it zooms in on the very worst of the what-ifs, without any filtering.

That's why Rob was stuck. The minions of Fear and Doubt had teamed up against him—to the point that he feared catastrophe for his family.

Fear was shouting, "You're going to fail!" Doubt was sneering, "You aren't good enough to succeed." Then they'd point directly at him and yell, "Give up that stupid dream!!!"

But it was all false. Deep down, Rational Rob knew this, but emotions were speaking at the moment, and he'd become their punching bag.

This is typically when Fear's first cousin, Worry, steps up. He's on the same team as Fear, only he's more subtle. And he plays the long game. He prefers to spar with you endlessly, aiming a quiet barrage of questions and concerns at you until you have headaches, ulcers, or insomnia. Yet he offers no solutions. He'll let you walk around with low-grade fear always under the surface unless you wake up and send him home.

What all the members of the Legion of Doom—Fear, Doubt, and Pride—have in common is a disregard for what's true. They could not care less about facts. They're after our assumptions, our emotions, our imaginations. If they can capture those—so we treat every worry as valid and imagine every alert as a crisis—they win the match, forcing another dramatic confrontation.

But it doesn't have to be that way. You can change the momentum almost instantly. You'll have to quit taking their words at face value and start asking some tough questions. But I'm telling you, if you'll give yourself ninety seconds at the mention of a threat, your emotion will usually dissipate enough for you to discern, *Is this real, or am I being played?* and regain the advantage.

Speaker and author Tony Evans said, "Feelings have no intellect. They are real and powerful, but they do not think. . . . Align your actions to the truth rather than responding in your feelings, and you will find peace, calm, and a life of stable wisdom."[36] Truth will save the day. We must fight back with the truth by taking these villains to court, where every bad guy belongs.

Make Your Case

Think of any area of your life where you're struggling to get started on something important. It doesn't have to be job-related. It could be the decision to move cross-country, go back to school, get married, have kids, tackle your debt, or buy a home. What threat or threats keep running through your mind?

Can you hear the enemies of Fear, Doubt, or Pride now? What are they saying?

Let's put their statements on the witness stand using this three-part process:

1. *Write down the specific thought.* What bad things could happen?
2. *Put each statement on trial.* Deconstruct it. How likely is it that the threat will happen *really*? What would have to be true for the worst-case scenario to become a reality?

3. *Counter the lie with the truth.* Play out the opposite of each lie: What good things will happen?

I heard this quote a while back and it stuck out to me: "Stating your fears out loud helps diffuse them. It's like turning the light on in a dark room."[37] A jolt of truth is what gets you going again. You know how a dazed boxer is revived with smelling salts? One good whiff of the truth and the fog lifts. You shift from *What if?* to *What is?* . . . and suddenly you see a clear path out of the fight and on to your climb.

Do you see how this works?

Rob's "truth" wasn't reliable. It was *his* truth, not *the* truth. He'd been listening to the threats of his enemies for so long that he believed them. His strength was depleted, and his imagination was shut down.

To gain the upper hand, he had to stop paying attention to what the villains were saying and start defending himself. *The* truth is always our best defense.

Was his family really going to be homeless? Would he ever let them starve? Not on his life! He'd have to do an entire list of dumb things for that to happen—none of which he was going to do.

He wasn't about to let his loved ones down. And you know what? As soon as he came out of the corner swinging, those villains turned tail and ran. He just needed to stand up to them and hit back with some hard truth.

The day he and I talked, Rob was able to expose these villains for the liars they are, calling them out one by one. Then he countered with a flurry of truth. By the time Rob was done, he had everything he needed—an entire list of strategies for the *real* concerns of getting started:

- He and his wife had financial stability. They weren't going to be homeless.
- He *did* have what it takes to succeed in real estate.
- He had a mission that he knew he must complete.

Rob could do *all of the things*. And he could start now. He wasn't cornered after all. He only felt that way because he believed a few lies.

A revitalized Rob saw that, by punching back, he would win. He'd be doing work he always wanted to do to fund a dream that would impact the lives of young people and leave a legacy. It was GAME OVER for Team Fear, Doubt, and Pride. He was about to knock them out.

Relieved and Revived

Stories like Rob's fire me up! Do you believe that you can overcome the enemies of progress?

It's so important to state out loud the enemy narrative that's going through your head. Two things happen instantly: First, you see how farfetched it is—laughable even. Second, as soon as you expose it, calling out the lie as a lie, the villains start shrinking and shriveling up like the Wicked Witch in *The Wizard of Oz*.

Confronting the lie reminds you: "I'm actually going to accomplish this. I have a path. I have hope."

The Stories Villains Tell Us

Now that you've been introduced to the three enemies that keep us from getting started, we're going to explore what each villain likes to tell us—what his favorite narrative is—so you'll recognize their voices more quickly.

Fear

She's one of the world's most famous singers, with two of the top-selling albums of all time—and she is terrified to walk on stage every time she performs in front of a live audience. In fact, Adele's nerves once got to her so badly that she tried to leave a concert venue by crawling out the fire escape!

The anxiety is real, people! Professional performers call it *stage fright* or *performance anxiety*, but anyone in any career can experience this. You know it as well as I do. Anyone can find themselves afraid to step out and get started, in spite of knowing they were made for doing what they're about to do.

What is Fear telling *you* about getting started? See if any of these statements sound familiar:

> *"I have no idea how this is all going to happen."*
> *"I really want to pursue my dream but it's too risky."*

This is what *fear of the unknown* sounds like. The unknowns can be almost anything, but the uncertainty is what gets to us. We like a sure thing. Getting started doesn't have many of those.

"What if this doesn't work out?"
"If this doesn't work, it will destroy me financially."

Total destruction isn't in any responsible person's future. But *fear of failure* can easily convince us that it is. We could "What if?" till the cows come home. The problem is, doing that keeps us stuck in the ring, distant from our dream.

"I'm going to let everyone down!"
"What will others think?"

This is "peer fear," as I call it. *Fear of judgment.* We're afraid people will either look at us differently, be disappointed, or think we're being reckless fools, putting ourselves or our family at needless risk.

Theresa's husband was on board with her desire to leave a successful corporate career to become a travel agent. His support and income eased her concerns, and knowing she'd have less stress and be home with her daughter more also helped. It was her friends and colleagues that she was worried about. If she'd said it once, she'd said it twenty times: "Everybody is going to call me crazy. . . ."

"I'm not good at promoting myself."
"I don't want to put myself out there."

This fear, the *fear of rejection*, turns us inward more than any of them: *I won't reach my dream because something is wrong with me.*

As we're trying to move forward, a host of factors may be hindering us—real circumstances beyond our control—yet we assume every no is personal. Deep down, what pains us most is feeling that *we're* not enough—or fearing we won't be. That's the message rejection sends. Because those wounds have cut so deep in the past, Fear often hits us hardest here.

Jenny bought into the lie so long ago she was buried in it.

This incredibly talented young lady knew early on what her dream job was and went after it. She'd earned a degree and found a great job in her hometown, working as a prop designer. Truly, it was her dream job. She'd built up a large network of connections there—but then she met a guy from South America. They fell in love, and she left everything behind to move overseas to be with him.

After their divorce a year later, she returned to the States—bringing with her a heavy load of sadness and a strong fear of rejection. Fast-forward eight years, and she was drifting from job to job, feeling the best she could do was just get by. She still grieved both the guy who broke her heart and the dream job she'd given up to be with him. Ultimately, Fear was alive and well—and holding her back.

Her ex's rejection had convinced her that she would be rejected everywhere else. That there were no second chances for somebody who throws away a great thing. But it simply wasn't true. She, just like anyone else, could do a reset. All she needed was a plan to get back to the place where her dream had begun.

Putting Fear's lies on trial reminded her of who she was and who she could be again. Past the pain was the Jenny who absolutely knew her passion, her mission, and her talent. She'd proven it before. She was due for an encore!

Doubt

Our second villain is Doubt, and his attacks circle around time, our destiny, and our ability. While Fear is busy distracting us with threats of what can hurt us, Doubt whispers, "Look at you and how weak/ill-prepared/undeserving you are."

He works all the inside angles, messing with our emotions and expertly building on the negative to demoralize and defeat us. At the hint of any slight failure or criticism, Doubt adds to the pile: "See? This is too hard for you. You're never going to make it." Statements like these may have no basis in reality, but as soon as they become a fact *for you*, you'll be tempted to give up and let your plans die.

The biggest doubts that people have when they're getting started are about time, ability, and destiny. Have you ever said these things?

"It's too late for me. I missed the boat."
"I guess this isn't meant to happen for me."

Some people think they waited too long or started too late—or they're just plain too old and time has run out. That was totally me early on. At any age, though, if you've had a few false starts or been rejected enough times, it's easy to think that the universe is sending you a message to pack up and go home.

"I'm not sure I can pull this off."
"Maybe I'm deceiving everybody, including myself, and I really can't do the job!"

Yikes! I have been paralyzed by those voices before!

A couple of years ago, I was on a business trip in Orlando when someone from the Ramsey team called and said, "Sirius XM wants to do a Dave Ramsey channel, and there's talk of you doing a show that will lead into Dave's."

I'd been at Ramsey for three years at this point. I was working toward a national show, but this call was totally unexpected and way ahead of the schedule I had in my mind. Still, I was *stoked*! I'd dreamed of having a national show for years.

Somewhere, though, between that phone call and the signing of the deal, it hit me: *Uh-oh! What am I thinking? I've never done a show that is 100 percent caller driven before. What if I'm awful at it?*

Wouldn't you know it? The deal went fast. Really fast. The performer in me was jumping up and down with excitement. At the same time, I was daunted, painfully aware that if I failed on Sirius, there probably wouldn't be a restart. I might even ruin my chances of ever getting another show.

This was Doubt, trying his best to discourage me.

I'm going to keep it real with you—the start of the show was rough. In a matter of weeks, we had to come up with the format. The music. Write the opener. Develop the material. It was a lot in a short amount of time. I wouldn't want anyone to hear the first few months of the show now . . . but I started. And as I went along, I learned more and got better. Doubt lost that round, but he put up a tough fight, dogging me every step of the way.

Pride

Our third villain, Pride, is crafty. He uses our own ego, insecurities, or impatience against us so that we stop ourselves from starting.

Here's one of his telltale signs: *What will people think of me?* Rather than the pressure or disappointment of peer fear, Pride is about our own status in the eyes of others—about keeping up appearances.

This version of Pride tends to rear its head with people who are farther along in their careers or switching careers later in life, like I did. After my disastrous demo at Turner Sports, I had to swallow my pride and go to broadcasting school—me, a husband and father of three— with a group of guys and gals who were still battling pimples.

Nobody wants to be perceived as going backwards. Or as failing to make it by the time others have made it. But Pride will tell us that's exactly what's at risk. Here's what it sounds like:

"I've already paid my dues."
"I shouldn't have to prove myself. My past work speaks for itself."

Pride can show his face anytime we're having to step back or start over. Choosing to give up your position for the sake of your dream is a noble thing. But Pride turns it into a blow to our ego.

For older workers in particular, the very idea of getting started toward a new dream means you're giving up something and having to gear up again at a time when you hoped to be at the top of your career. I had to give up a successful radio show in Georgia to have a shot at my dream job in Nashville. I went back to holding the microphone for others after writing a book and being behind the mic myself for a few years. It wasn't easy for me.

Some people respond with humility and a desire to learn the ropes. But Pride will make us feel resistant. And if we're treated like a rookie instead of given the respect we know we've earned, it can be even worse. *That* can feel like an insult. It's like having to re-audition for a stage role you've played for years.

Naturally, we'd like to be recognized for what we've accomplished. A certain level of that is healthy. We should have pride in work well done. But Pride the Villain will want to push you too far, until you're bitter.

"I'm being overlooked."

Sometimes you really are being overlooked—but sometimes you're just being impatient or acting entitled.

Joy Bryant, my favorite teacher of all time, taught speech and drama at my high school. In my junior year, she cast me as Christopher Wren in the school play, Agatha Christie's *The Mousetrap*. Prior to our first real rehearsal, she had clearly communicated to all of us that we were supposed to know our lines.

Right up front I need to admit that I wanted to be the lead, Giles Ralston. My desire had nothing to do with Giles's actual part. The character was pretty straight-laced, the owner and manager of an inn. I wanted the lead simply because, from my teenaged "performer" perspective, that meant top billing and the most attention.

It's obvious to me now that Mrs. Bryant cast me as Wren for a reason, knowing I'd love getting the laughs of this wacky, hyperactive character. But until I played Wren in front of a live audience, I didn't see the gift in it. So as rehearsals began, I was still feeling hurt by the perceived snub and a little sorry for myself. I slacked off in my preparation—something I wouldn't have done with the Giles role. Wren came naturally enough to me that my pride decided I wasn't going to sweat it.

Fast-forward to the first day of full rehearsals, *Act I, Scene 1.*

I dropped my very first line.

I blew it again moments later.

After the third fail, Mrs. Bryant stopped the practice, walked up on stage, called me over by the curtains, and quietly but firmly said, "Ken, I know you're going to get the lines. And you know you're going to. But everyone else here has theirs memorized. You don't. You're not ready, and you're slowing us down. You need to nail it now, not later. Grab your script and learn the lines. Start taking this seriously."

Ouch! Did that ever sting! But she was right. I carried my script with me the rest of the practice—the only cast member that needed to. And I learned my lesson. After that day, I didn't dare show up to rehearsal unprepared.

In this form, Pride tells us, "This is about you. You deserve better." When we don't get our way, we sometimes pout and let down in our performance—the adult version of a temper tantrum. What we're missing is that not only are we hurting the team, but we're also sabotaging ourselves. Nothing can prevent you from giving it your all except for your pride.

"I've got it. I don't need any help."

The most valuable question people never ask is, "Will you help me?" Whether it's help while you're getting qualified or for something else entirely, not asking for help or refusing help when it's offered are Pride's most obvious symptoms.

I get it. We don't want someone thinking we can't get our work done. But if you were being overcome by ocean waves, wouldn't you want lifeguards to come save you? If you were in some kind of trouble, wouldn't you call 911? Pride says you don't need anyone else—that you're faster on your own. Humility says collaboration will be the key to your greatest successes.

Keep Fighting for the Ultimate Win

Fear, Doubt, and Pride don't ever retire. They will keep picking fights your entire life—in many areas of your life, not just your career. It always makes me think of the John Wick movies, where the bad guys keep coming at Keanu Reeves's character.

So what's the good news when the bad guys keep coming at John Wick from all corners? Wick always wins. You can overcome these villains each time using the three-part process I've given you. You may get knocked down a few times. You may get a bloody nose. But the truth will beat the bad guys every time, and it will keep beating them as often as you need it.

The villains we face remind me of patriot Patrick Henry's words about America's enemy as the Revolutionary War was ramping up:

They tell us, sir, that we are weak; unable to cope with so formidable an adversary. But when shall we be stronger? Will it be the next week, or the next year? . . . Shall we gather strength by irresolution and inaction. . . . until our enemies shall have bound us hand and foot? Sir, we are not weak if we make a proper use of those means which the God of nature hath placed in our power.[38]

If today isn't your day, then when? Don't you think it's time? When you have Truth on your side, nothing will be able to keep you from getting started toward your dream job. Nothing can stop you from breaking through the opposition and living your dream like no one else.

This is one of those gut-check moments, where the coach is calling you onto the field—and you either go or you don't.

Go catch the dream, champion! Fight past these troublemakers, and let's get on with the good stuff! Haven't you waited long enough?

Chapter 7 Takeaways

Remember This

Everything you've done up to this point is useless if you don't start!

You Got This

This is not the first time you have done something new.

Do This

Review the process for filtering the voices of Fear, Doubt, and Pride.

8

Start the Right Way

With an enormous mountain like Everest, what surprises me is not how few people make it to the peak but how many drop out before they arrive at base camp!

The mountain can be accessed from two different countries, Nepal or Tibet. Yet with no direct flights, it takes anywhere from several days to two weeks of additional travel and hiking for would-be climbers to reach base camp.

Of those who come to Asia each year with Everest in their sights, only about 10 percent will get as far as base camp. For a number of reasons, most people quit their journey during this time.

Why do I tell you that? Because there's actually something incredibly significant about reaching base camp. According to the Himalayan Database, which tracks all kinds of numbers about the world's highest mountain each year, those who actually make it above Everest's base camp have a great summit rate. On the Nepal side in 2018, three in four of the climbers "who got above base camp . . . went on to summit." From the Tibet side, two in three who got past base camp reached the peak.[39]

Those are such encouraging odds! Now that you're at base camp, you just have to start, and chances are very good that you'll be one of the success stories taking selfies at the peak. So let's talk about how to make the best start possible.

Just Start

Getting qualified was the hardest stage for me because I was so impatient. But getting started? I was all about it! I was finally doing something that felt relevant to the dream!

It felt like the first hill of a roller coaster. A little terrifying, sure. And yet I was relieved and elated to finally be on the ride after paying for my ticket and standing in line for so long.

My first live broadcast was as unremarkable as it could get, yet I was wide awake emotionally. I didn't care that I was doing play-by-play at a high school football game being broadcast on the internet or that the only two people listening were the kid sitting next to me in the booth and my wife! *I didn't care, because I was on my way!*

I laugh now, because I was down on the field before the game, interviewing the coaches like I was doing play-by-play for the Super Bowl. You've never seen bigger "So what?" stares than the ones I got that night. I couldn't help it, though. Because I was so fired up, opportunities like this felt like Christmas morning.

That's what I want for you: to love your work so much that your excitement overrides your fears. Like pregame jitters, you're nervous but excited.

Those are good nerves. Performance nerves.

Stepping out and getting started will usually reduce them. But what if they don't?

I like blogger Shannon Ables's perspective on the mixed emotions of a moment like this: "When you are fearful or scared it is because you actually have no evidence that you can or can't do it." This is "all the more reason to try," she urges, because while "you have no proof that you will succeed, . . . *you have no proof that you won't either.*"[40]

The key, says Ables, is believing more resolutely that you can rather than you can't. So what do you believe? That you can or you can't? As long as you're more convinced that you *can* accomplish what you've set out to do, you will succeed.

Notice she didn't say you have to be 100 percent convinced, just *more* convinced of success than failure.[41] To me, that feels totally doable. Even on a bad day, I can probably manage 51 percent belief that I can do what I'm setting out to do. How about you?

Thanks to everything we clarified and verified through all those actions in Stage 1, we also have the assurance of knowing *what's true* about us: our talent, our passion, our mission, our purpose, our sweet spot. That ought to boost our courage as well.

I'm not denying the difficulties of the climb. You're attempting to top a mountain after all. But if you've gotten this far, then you undoubtedly have what it takes to reach your dream job. This is your moment! You were put on this earth to do this! Stop putting it off—and start!

The Size of Your Steps

What size should the first step be? You're going to love this: the first step can be the smallest.

I'm not sure my first step was even a step. It was more like a shuffle.

You know what I did for my very first hired gig in my dream career? I introduced clowns and a mime at a city festival. The high point was when I exchanged an air high five with the mime. Now that I think about it, my first step was a stubbed toe.

Between that glamorous gig and the radio job in Atlanta, I did everything I could think of: public speaking, emceeing, podcasting. When I say podcasting, I mean in its frontier years—when almost no one was interested in staking a claim in that media wilderness, and there was no platform to be had. My studio was a sound booth about the size of a coat closet, with no air conditioning, in a warehouse in Georgia. And if you've ever been to Georgia in the summer, you know that "sweltering" is the temperature at four o'clock in the morning. Early on, success was an audience numbering in the low hundreds. *Millions* wasn't on anybody's radar. Talk about humble beginnings.

It didn't matter, though. I knew that broadcasting was the mountain I wanted to climb. And these were the steps I had to take.

There's a gem of a verse tucked away in the Bible that reminds us never to "despise," or look down on, the day of small beginnings.[42] What a powerful word! Small starts are nature's way. Oak trees originate from acorns. Colts grow to be racehorses. Little leaguers become major leaguers. One sentence becomes an entire book. Don't worry about the size of the steps. Just keep stepping.

The Important First Step

She was a makeup artist with a powerful dream. After volunteering at a nonprofit for homeless women and getting to know some of those beautiful souls, Whitney was inspired to do more. She was on fire to create a nonprofit that gave free makeovers to homeless women who were trying to re-enter the job market.

Her idea was to sell makeup and makeovers but with a Toms Shoes–type twist. Instead of "you buy a pair and we'll donate a pair," she wanted to give a service for each service or product bought. So every time a customer bought makeup, Whitney would do a makeover for a homeless client.

Speaking for nearly every one of us who has ever been standing at the base of our mountain, wondering how to get to the peak, she asked, "What should I do next? It's hard for me to narrow down my next step."

One of the main reasons people don't start is because they think it has to be a perfect start. Or a flashy start. It doesn't.

Make it a good start—the right start for you.

St. Francis of Assisi said it better than I ever could: "Start by doing what's necessary, then do what's possible, and suddenly you are doing the impossible." We will cover some steps for would-be entrepreneurs like Whitney at the end of this chapter, but right now I want to show you how to take that necessary *first* step—with your heart and head working together to set the course for your dream.

Friends, there is such power in stepping out of the boat! Once Peter the apostle's mind and heart were aligned, *he walked on water*.[43] But not until he left the safety of the boat.

The first step is the most important step. It relieves some of your jitters, giving you a task to focus on instead. It also gives you confidence to take additional steps. So have a little faith and do what's necessary right now: *deliberately choose a job that puts you directly on course to your dream.* Then, as you're offered promotions or other positions, do it again and again until you've reached the goal.

Like choosing a hiking trail at a national park, you can't entirely predict what you'll encounter as you go, but I'll give you the trail markers to watch for so you won't get lost.

The Right Start

To start right, you need to choose

> **the right path** . . .
> in **the right place** . . .
> at **the right pace** . . .
> always keeping **the right perspective**.

Keep in mind, these four trail markers will apply to every job from this point on until you end up exactly where you want to be.

Trail Marker #1: The Right Path

Christy was doing what she loved—event marketing—for a company that she didn't love so much. She constantly felt undervalued and overlooked, in big ways and small, and this was reinforced with each paycheck. It was a regular reminder that she was significantly under-paid compared to peers who were doing the same kind of work at other companies.

Something better was ahead for her, though. One of the companies she applied to a couple of years before had started actively recruiting her. (It's always nice when they realize what they passed up!) Besides being in the same sector of her industry and suggested by a mentor of hers, this job had something else going for it: the employer was offering Christy a 50 percent raise. She was worried, though, because the new job was in a different area of marketing. "Maybe I'll love the work," she said. "But I can't say for sure. What if I don't?"

She was considering staying at her current company when they listed a position that was absolutely in Christy's sweet spot. She knew it the second she read the job description. "It was a step above what I was doing," she explained. "But then they told me, 'You're too young.'"

As disappointing as this was, it was also the confirmation she needed. It was time to leave the nest and try her wings elsewhere. Now that she'd seen what that next sweet-spot position looked like, Bella could use that information to evaluate the new opportunity. Did this other position have all the things going for it? Was it only a good job, or was it a sweet-spot job?

The right start to your dream job involves choosing the right path—*the most direct path*—to your goal. Think of each job you take as another stepping-stone across a river. You're trying to cross as quickly as possible without slipping. You do this by selecting jobs that keep you in your sweet spot, aligned with your unique role.

Remember, your role can be expressed in a variety of jobs across different industries. So don't get caught up in job titles or whether a company is well known. You can be in an entry-level position at a small business in a small town and still be in your sweet spot. Take the job that keeps you in your sweet spot.

Make your decisions based on your answers in Stage 1: *Will this position let me use what I do best and love to do most to produce results that matter to me?* This is your decision-making grid for your entire professional journey. At every stage of your path to meaningful work—at every "T" in the road—I want you to tell yourself, "But not outside my sweet spot . . ."

Two Good Paths

Every once in a while, life hands you two good choices, two seemingly great sweet-spot jobs, either of which could catapult you toward your dream job. I try to keep it simple in these situations. To evaluate the right path for you, run each opportunity, Job A and Job B, thoroughly through the pros and cons. Which one gives you the best chance of moving farther and faster?

Is there a clear winner? Great! Go with it! If not, you can put it to the test as we did in chapter 2. I call it a heart check, but a lot of people refer to it as a gut check. It's the same process.

Scientists have actually done research on the reliability of our gut. In one study they monitored the heart rates of master chess players during a chess match, and they noticed that the players' pulses spiked three times:

- When the clock was running out on their current play.
- When they saw their opponent making a bad move and the players realized they had a chance to win.
- When they were making a bad move. This is when their heart rate changed the most.

In each case, their heart signaled that something was going on. Those gut feelings that increase our pulse are just as relevant in decision-making as the information we gather.

My rule of thumb for career choices and life choices is: Follow your brain on simple decisions. Listen to your heart on more complex decisions.

Your heart will guide you to the right path. It *does* know best whether or not you have the words to explain it. Trust what it tells you.

Trail Marker #2: The Right Place

Life's too short for a workplace environment that depletes and diminishes us. You need a place where you can launch your career and grow toward your dream. Look for these criteria as you're deciding where to get started:

1. Do they have an "opportunity ladder"? What's above the position you're applying for? Does that keep you on your path? You want to start out somewhere with a clear ladder for climbing that also promotes from within.

2. Do they invest in their employees, offering high-quality training that produces great performers? In Soledad O'Brien's early days as a TV reporter in San Francisco, a producer advised her to get some practice at being a show anchor. He said that someday she'd be called on to fill that role, and she should be ready.

O'Brien went to her boss at the station and asked for a chance. His response was quick: "We have enough women anchors; we don't need any more."

That conversation showed her this was not a place where she could grow her skills. So she resigned and found another station that would train her for where she wanted to be, not just for the job she was in.[44]

Sometimes the no we receive means "not now." But sometimes it means "not here." How seriously do the companies on your list take employee development? What kind of success do their current and past employees achieve? You can go to ramseysolutions.com/career-advice/interview-guide and find our Interview Guide, which gives you questions to ask to get at some of these answers.

3. How healthy is the culture? At this stage, you're trying to avoid toxic or negative cultures. Either type of workplace confuses people about their calling and brings down their morale. You'll feel like you're going backwards even though you're supposed to be working your way up. It's worth your time to do a little research and build a file on any company you're considering.

Of course, this begs a follow-up question: How do you learn whether a company has a healthy culture before you join it? You're going to be spending the majority of your waking hours in this place, so make good use of these resources:

- *See what former employees are saying on sites like Indeed.* If you find only a handful of negative scores and remarks among many positive ones, then chances are you're hearing from the rusty wheels who probably aren't happy anywhere. But if there are a lot of overly negative comments, pay attention to that.

- *Do a social media search.* See what's being said there by any and all who know the company you're considering.

- *Ask around among your connections.* What's the word on the street? What do the people who work there say? Try to connect with current employees. If they don't like it, they'll be eager to say what they really think. If they love it, they'll be excited to evangelize and tell you what's so great about the company.

- *Check the media coverage.* What's being reported in the press? Explore beyond the mainstream media (local network news and newspapers). Look at independent sources—business publications, industry magazines—that have interviewed executives or employees. What sense do you get about the company's values, priorities, and treatment of people?

- *What do their customers and vendors say?* Check out customer reviews as well as sites like the Better Business Bureau. A company that disregards these people will disregard its employees. Again, though, look for the general consensus. One or two bad-apple reports don't necessarily mean the entire place is rotten. But lots of negative reports from various sources are something to be wary of.

No one source is going to give you the answer you need, but pay attention to the overall impression you get. The good companies will rise to the top.

Trail Marker #3: The Right Pace

I can sum up the wrong pace for starting in two words: too soon!

So many people move on to the next thing too soon. As you're moving from position to position in Stage 4, your best approach is to pace yourself. The future will come to you if you go at it step by step. Let's talk about what this looks like in different situations.

Lewis had been teaching music to elementary school students for six years. "It was really a dream job at first: dream location, great place, great staff, great pay," he said. But lately he'd been losing interest. Like ivy on a fence, a slow-growing creep had been stifling his spirit.

The music was still in him, even if the classroom wasn't cutting it anymore: "I'd been volunteering in the music ministry at my church. I'd been thinking I'd really love to write songs and make ministry a full-time thing." Yet he hesitated to leave his current job, where all his training was.

By this point in the book, you probably know how to advise Lewis: *Buddy, don't stay in a line of work that you aren't passionate about! There are other ways you can play your role!*

Lewis will have to take some steps to get qualified, but my main qualifier for him in this moment is to create a strong exit strategy.

Prepare for his future on the side while continuing to teach—and don't leave teaching until he can walk triumphantly into a paid ministry position.

That's the right pace for when your dream changes.

What about when you're in a toxic culture and you think you can't stand one more second of it? That's when the temptation to move fast will be strongest. But cliff jumpers, beware! Without something to jump *to*, you're jumping off a cliff to certain disaster.

If you dread your job for any reason, go find another one. Have that in your back pocket before you hand in your notice.

Except for situations of abuse, harassment, or illegal activity, you can and should put up with your current job long enough to get another job. Having a jerk boss or rude coworkers isn't an emergency that warrants living off your savings for two or three months. You only hurt yourself by leaping too soon.

I want you stepping off the dock onto a boat, not into the water. That's the ideal job transition.

Entrepreneurs feel the same pressure but for a different reason: they want profits or prominence fast. But if you're taking the first yes you get, it can spell disaster.

From Mr. Impatient himself, I can say to you what I've had to tell myself: *Bro, there's twenty-six miles to go and you're sprinting! Slow your roll or you're gonna hurt yourself!*

Chad's brand-new video-production business was moving at warp speed, and he couldn't have felt luckier if he'd struck oil. His very first client had proposed a major project *and* a multiyear contract! How often does that happen?

He was on it!

Chad and his client contact, Larry, had firmed up a shoot schedule quickly. So Chad went out and bought all the equipment he'd need: cameras, lighting pieces, computers, editing software. It was money he didn't have, but once the contract was signed, those costs would be covered.

He was so excited he told all his friends, "I'm doing this. It's going to be great!"

The filming started, and everything was proceeding like clockwork. But then came the phone call.

"I'm really, really sorry, man," Larry began. Chad could hear the dejection in his voice. "My boss changed his mind. Said he'll pay you for the work you've done so far, but he's pulling the plug. It's a no-go."

Just like that, it was over. Larry was a good guy, a nice guy, but he wasn't the decision guy. The contract wasn't coming.

As awful as Larry felt, Chad was wrecked. He'd hit the gas pedal on a promise, and now he had no choice but to shut down his business and sell off all the equipment. The financial toll was bigger than he wanted to admit. The emotional toll was probably greater. This would take him a very, very long time to dig out of.

Of course we want instant success, but building a business isn't the hundred-meter dash. Instead, create a plan to outlast the competition and go the distance.

Think of the difference between how endurance runners and sprinters start a race. Sprinters spend months training for a perfectly executed, carefully timed burst from the blocks that will shave micro-seconds off their race. The marathoners? They show up in a gaggle and meander toward the starting line. Your best chance at success as an entrepreneur is to start small and grow slow.

Trail Marker #4: The Right Perspective

Each of the trail markers we've looked at so far will give you good perspective as you get started. This final trail marker is especially important, though, for keeping you on course when circumstances set you back. Those are the times you need the right perspective most of all.

As I was trying to break into radio, I worked for free several hours a week at a large sports-talk station in Atlanta. It was a good chance for me to gain more experience and be around other radio people.

For six months, I fetched coffee for hosts, conducted show research, and screened calls. As I made friends with several hosts, they began putting me on air to comment and report from live games.

I was experiencing what seemed like good momentum until I called the program director one day to request a press pass. Sam was the program director who had green-lighted my volunteer internship a month earlier, and I needed the pass for a big story the midday hosts had asked me to cover.

He refused.

I pressed him, asking him to reconsider his decision. Sam combusted, "Ken, stop pushing me on this! You're not an employee! I can't approve your press pass. You shouldn't even be on air anyway. You don't have the talent to make it in a top-ten market. You need to move on."

I hung up the phone with my head spinning and my heart sinking. Suddenly everything I'd worked for was gone, swallowed up in a fog of rejection. Sam's words not only crushed my spirit, but I think I experienced every lizard brain emotion at the same time: I was scared. I wanted to run. And I was paralyzed.

For the next several days, I replayed everything I'd said and done while on the job. I questioned myself, my worth, my discernment, and worried that I'd ruined my chances to achieve this dream. *Was it over, just like that? Was Sam right about me?*

One day, I was mowing my lawn and pulling weeds. Evidently the yardwork helped quiet my lizard brain enough that I could finally start sorting the truth from the lies. With a clearer head, I realized: *I have options*. I could let Sam decide my career path, or I could redirect and try a new door rather than kicking at one that was slammed shut.

What did I know for sure? I had passion for broadcasting. It fit my mission, and by the confirmation I'd gotten from other people I'd worked with, I had the talent. If I kept at it, I knew I could get better. I also acknowledged something just as important: I liked sports radio, but I didn't love it enough to spend my life doing it.

With the smoke and mirrors out of my way, my mind was set free, and I could see a different path unfolding. That day, the idea was born for a podcast, which gave me some additional exposure and connections and became the foundation for my first book, *One Question*. That podcast kept me on the path until I arrived at the talk-radio station in Gainesville, Georgia . . . and you've read the rest of the story.

In hindsight, maybe Sam was concerned that I would eventually want to be paid since I was getting some airtime. Or maybe he felt I was overstepping my bounds by going on air at all. I'll probably never know.

I can still recall the sting when I think about how it all played out. Sam's rejection hurt a lot, and it scared me on many levels. I had to sort through each one, a layer at a time. But it didn't knock me down for the count. Instead, it fueled my resolve to redirect and start moving more strategically in the direction of my dreams.

The right perspective as you get started is to always, no matter what, keep moving. When the unexpected happens, keep moving. When your own version of Sam tells you that you aren't cut out for your dream job, keep moving. When you're eaten up by Fear or Doubt, keep moving. When you're tired and discouraged and don't know what to do, *keep moving*.

Signs and Second-Guessing

As you get started on your climb and move from position to position (at the right pace, of course!), when the villains show up or unexpected change happens, you'll almost inevitably second-guess yourself: *Am I really supposed to do this? Maybe this is a sign I'm headed the wrong way.*

Here's what I want you to know: it *is* a sign. But if you've gotten clear on everything to this point, and you've been doing the work, the sign isn't saying, "Turn around and go home." Instead, it's saying, "Time to do something different."

You don't give up. (That's what the villains are hoping for!) You *do* retreat to clarity. And you *do* continue looking for alternate routes. The desired future is still ahead if you'll stay the course. It simply may not be the exact course or timeline you imagined.

We forget that the struggle actually makes us stronger. Do you know the story of the man who was out walking and spotted a small cocoon attached to a leaf? He saw the edges of the chrysalis moving and realized the butterfly was struggling to break free. Wanting to help the butterfly, the man gently pried open the cocoon. But instead of the butterfly gracefully flying out of the opening, it fell to the ground and died. Why? Because without the struggle to leave the cocoon, the butterfly's wings never fully developed. The struggle is what strengthens us for the next stage.

Every caterpillar needs the struggle in order to be transformed into a butterfly. So do we. So keep moving, keep fighting. This is the essence of *resilience*, the ability to bounce back from setbacks. And you have the resilience you need. *Psychology Today* reports: "Resilience is the rule, not the exception. . . . We are designed to overcome, not to succumb."[45]

In other words, a comeback isn't just a nice way to end a movie— it's what we're made for! One of the great scenes in movie history is from *Apollo 13*, which recounts a real-life crisis within the US space program in April 1970. Apollo astronauts Jim Lovell, Jack Swigert, and Fred Haise were supposed to land on the moon, and would have been the third flight crew in US history to do so, but their lunar landing was aborted due to an oxygen-tank rupture. This unexpected event did more than disrupt the mission. It put the astronauts' lives at risk.

For these three brave men to have any chance of making it back to earth alive, the team on the ground in Houston had to improvise and coordinate new procedures for a situation none of them had ever planned on.

You'll have to see the movie for yourself. But the telling moment comes when Ed Harris, who plays lead flight director Gene Kranz, overhears two NASA team members talking about the perils that the spacecraft and its crew are facing.

"The parachute situation, the heat shield, the . . . trajectory, and the typhoon are just some of the variables—"

The other man cuts him off. "I know what the problems are, Henry. This could be the worst disaster NASA has ever experienced."

Kranz turns, stares at the second man, and says, "With all due respect, sir, I believe this is gonna be our finest hour."

You're made to overcome.

In the early stages of climbing to your professional pinnacle, you need to know you're made of the same unstoppable stuff as Kranz. Things will not go according to plan, *but you are built to bounce back.* Keep to the right path, the right place, the right pace, and the right perspective—and remember that Fear, Doubt, Pride, and the unexpected can only stop you if you let them.

Don't let them.

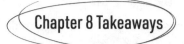

Remember This

No matter how big or how good it is, the
first step is the most important.

You Got This

You have prepared for this. It is your time!

Do This

Review the four trail markers in this chapter
and apply them to your path.

STAGE 5

Get Promoted up the Ladder

9

Win the Now to Get to the Next

They weren't hearing me!" Andrea declared. "I didn't want to leave, but I was becoming more and more frustrated because my leaders weren't recognizing my voice or ideas. Then the pandemic happened."

Was it a sign? Time to bail?

Sometimes during Stage 5—the Get Promoted stage of our journey—circumstances do point us in a new direction, and we promote ourselves by finding a better job in a better environment. But Andrea liked this job and the people she worked with. *And* she was thankful to still have a job. Her heart was to help the executives through this critical time, being part of the solution rather than jumping ship. So Andrea opted to step up and work to become the company's go-to person.

Really, what did she have to lose? *Even if my leaders don't see it, my colleagues will, and I'll earn a reputation for getting things done*, she reasoned. To her, that would be its own form of promotion.

The details of those first few months of the pandemic are a little fuzzy. There was lots of overtime, making sure her bosses had what they needed. What Andrea does remember clearly is how energizing get-it-done mode felt. Though her hours spiked to seventy hours a week and she was living on coffee and quick meals, she was excited to contribute in a bigger way. She also sensed a shift in the way she was being perceived.

Once the company was past the crisis phase, she asked her leadership for a meeting. "I'm on overload," she admitted, "though I've loved the extra responsibility. How can we make this work—keep the momentum going but with a more sustainable load?"

This time, her bosses heard her. And they responded by letting Andrea work from home. They also revised her job description, giving her focused tasks that fit her new role but that wouldn't burn her out.

Five months later, Andrea reported: "I've never been happier at work. Every single member of my executive team has recognized the quality and quantity of my work. We still have a long way to go, but I've earned tremendous credibility with the executives and my colleagues. Finally, I am seen for my value and my ideas!"

Game On!

You're in the arena now. The clock is running. Everyone is keeping score!

The top of the mountain seems closer than ever before. And it is! Stage 5—the Get Promoted stage—is where you start to break out from the crowd and climb the ladder. But the irony is that getting promoted isn't about the *next* . . . it's all about the *now*.

When you get to Stage 5, the temptation is to immediately start looking to the future and your next steps. Let me caution you, though: you never want to come in to a new job caring only about moving up. It's counterintuitive, I know, but being obsessed with the *next* at this phase of your journey will be your undoing. Instead, you get promoted by knocking it out of the park in your current position, as Andrea did. I call it *winning the now*. There is no *next* without being a champion right where you are.

Three Actions That Get You Promoted

Back in the day, when our grandparents were in their prime, workers were usually handed a promotion just for clocking in for a few years. Not anymore. Now you get promoted for what you do and who you are. In order to demonstrate that you're ready for the next level, focus on these three promotable actions in the *now*. Consider them the three rungs on your job ladder:

1. *Know your role.*
2. *Accept your role.*
3. *Maximize your role.*

A rung at a time, you take the ladder higher. And as you do, you'll get to where you want to be.

These three specific actions, along with the five character qualities that we'll explore in chapter 10, will make you a Most Valuable Player (MVP) on your team, regardless of which rung you're on. The *doing* gets you noticed. The *being* raises you above the crowd. Sometimes getting promoted means seeking the change you want, and sometimes it means being the change you seek. Either way, you can't *not* be successful if you're doing the right things every day.

Rung #1 on the Ladder: Know Your Role

You may be a diehard fan of your favorite NFL team, but I can guarantee you don't have this guy's jersey hanging in your closet—because the manufacturers don't sell his stuff. You probably don't even know his name. I'm talking about the long snapper on the kicking team. (For those of you who don't follow football, that's the dude who hikes the ball to the player who's holding it for the placekicker.)

As pro sports go, there's hardly a more thankless job. He's the team's minimum-wage earner, on the field for only seconds at a time, yet those brief appearances are often high pressure and make-or-break. Every scoring attempt involving a kick starts with him. A single mistake can get him fired—*just like that.* And in case that's not enough stress, a few wins or losses every season (sometimes the fate of the entire season!) will be decided by his handling of the snap in coordination with the holder and the kicker.

What makes these guys successful? They're super clear on their role: get the ball in the holder's hands. They go out and do it time and again, anonymous as they may be, for the team. Not just for themselves.

Now that you've been hired, the ball is in your hands. Your team is counting on you. Step up and take radical responsibility for *your* job. That's the first rung of the ladder. Whatever your position, you must know your role. Then you can do your role.

Ideally, you were learning your role even during the interview process, but once you're reporting to work, you have to know *exactly* what's expected of you in your current assignment. This starts with getting crystal clear on two priorities:

- Your job responsibilities
- The results that are expected of you

Ramsey Solutions has developed a one-sheet that outlines these two things. We call it a KRA or Key Results Area, and every employee reviews it with their leader. I can vouch for how useful this is. It really does help to know: "Okay, these are my assignments, and here are the results my leaders are looking for." You've been given a clear lane to drive in. Now you can carry out your work with excellence.

If this isn't something the company already does, you don't have to wait for them to adopt it. You're doing this for you. So write up a one-sheet yourself if you need to. List your responsibilities and your expected results as you understand them. Then sit down with your leader and ask, "How does my role fit into the team? How do I help our organization win?" Fine-tune it together, then go do it!

Getting promoted someday starts with knowing your role today. Learn your role so you can do it with excellence. On any given day, *you* could be one of the heroes who makes greatness happen.

Rung #2 on the Ladder: Accept Your Role

Now that you know your job, *do your job*. Happily. Accepting your role is all about embracing it. It's bringing the right attitude to work every day and finding ways to contribute to your team and the organization. Where you are today might not be your dream role, but remember, there's no *next* if you don't crush the *now*. How do you do this? Focus on three things:

- Having a grateful heart
- Honing your craft
- Evaluating your own performance, not others'

1. Have a grateful heart. Getting drafted and making the team was half the battle. You're in! You're on the ladder with the opportunity to go higher. Don't take it for granted when the work gets hard or you're feeling discouraged.

I recall a specific time during Stage 5 where I lost sight of this. After ten years of grinding just to get in the door at Ramsey Solutions, I still wasn't in the studio every day like I dreamed. Not even close. Dave did put me to work right away hosting events and occasional shows, and that was super cool. But it wasn't long before I was getting antsy again. I had assured people within the organization that I was ready and eager to be put in the game, but there were no signs of change.

Feeling especially impatient one night, I was venting to Stacy, and she said, "Ken, I totally get your frustration, but you need to remind yourself how excited you were a year and a half ago to take this position. And remember where you were five years ago. You're almost there."

Recalling where I'd come from gave me perspective, and with perspective came a gratitude that refueled my patience like a pit stop during a NASCAR race. *Perspective* means "seeing clearly"—taking off the glasses of expectation and seeing what is. I'd been so obsessed about the *next* that I was in danger of forfeiting my *now*. Had I stayed frustrated, I would've missed what I needed to learn to be ready for what was coming.

If you're feeling weary or frustrated today, take a fresh look at your situation. Not everybody makes it this far. You were *chosen* from a list of candidates (and maybe from a pool several hundred people deep). Your current company saw something special in you. Don't throw that away. Instead, give yourself some time to reflect on how far you've come. Be grateful for all your progress. You. Are. Almost. There!

2. Hone your craft. Accepting your role also means you're doing everything on your one-sheet with excellence. And excellence takes time and practice to develop. The first time I ever interviewed someone in a broadcast setting I got a jolt of motivation to keep improving myself and my interview skills. It was 2004, and I was preparing to interview Duke University basketball coach Mike Krzyzewski. The fact that I was sitting on the Blue Devils bench in Cameron Indoor Stadium, home to my favorite college basketball team, was hard enough to wrap my head around. But to be there to ask questions of this legendary coach in person was almost more than I could absorb.

Originally, Fox Sports commentator Bob Rathbun, one of my mentors, had been scheduled to do the interview, but he'd had to cancel. As Bob's copy editor for the segment, I knew what had been planned and so I was asked to fill in.

As Coach K entered the gym and was mic'd up for the interview, I was barely in my body. But after a few questions, we got in a good rhythm and I did what I'd prepared to do. As part of my research,

I'd read his book *Leading with the Heart*. He had mentioned in the book that he treats all his players "fair but not equal." I wanted him to unpack that a bit more, so I asked him to give us a picture, which he did, offering up a few examples with recent players.

A short time later, during a quick break while the camera crew changed tapes, Coach K told me, "I'm really enjoying this interview." That comment alone was enough to send me over the moon. But then he added, "You remind me of one of my best friends," and he named a renowned interviewer with a long history in television.

Those words both caught me off guard and lit a fire under me that day. I was so grateful that he saw potential in me—but I also knew I was nowhere near the caliber of his friend. I needed to become a better interviewer.

I walked out the doors of Cameron Stadium and began watching hours and hours of the pros at work: Larry King, Bob Costas, Barbara Walters, Roy Firestone. Their work inspired me to pitch a podcast about a year later to a leadership group I knew called Catalyst. The entire premise was to interview prominent people about leadership issues and concerns. That's where Elizabeth heard me. Remember her? She was my connection from chapter 2 who opened the broadcast radio doors for me. Catalyst also gave me the chance to occasionally emcee on stage at their events, which included interviewing people in front of a live audience. That's how I got to know Dave Ramsey.

There was no way I could predict the opportunities and connections that honing my craft would lead to, but becoming a better interviewer proved to be a hugely important part of accepting my role.

Whatever your calling—engineer, nurse, chef, marketer, electrician, landscaper, teacher—commit to being the absolute best you can be. And consider each day another great opportunity to practice.

3. *Evaluate your own performance, not others'*. How many times did our teachers tell us, "Keep your eyes on your own work," while we were taking a test? As you're accepting your role, I'm cautioning you to do the same in your job. Avoid comparing yourself with others. Keep your eyes on your own work.

Frankly, there's no winning the comparison game. The problem, according to author Andy Stanley, is that comparing always produces a loser: either somebody who is doing bigger or better than you—or worse than you. But what's the point of comparing? How does that serve you or them?

It doesn't. Turning your camera to capture someone else's performance won't lift you up the ladder. If anything, it can stall you at the current rung or, worse, pull you backwards in discouragement or jealousy. Put the camera away. The only person you should be looking at is *the you of yesterday*.

Are you more focused at work than you were last week? Are you a bolder leader than you were last month? Did you sell more this year than you did last year? *These* are worthwhile questions to reflect on. If the answer is yes, you're making progress—no matter what anyone around you is doing.

Instead of comparing, think of *measuring*. Those two things might sound the same, but there's a difference. Measuring focuses on healthy self-improvement. You can measure your work performance against your job description and expectations, not someone else's. You can measure the progress of your goals. You can measure the work you do today against the standard you set yesterday. Ask yourself where you won today and where you lost and analyze why. Then write down a couple of ways you intend to win tomorrow. You against you. As it should be.

Rung #3 on the Ladder: Maximize Your Role

Know your role, accept your role, and in time, you'll be maximizing your role.

To earn a promotion, you must go above and beyond your current responsibilities. No surprise there. But let me offer you this advice: do the work of your next job before you get the job. As long as you're not overstepping boundaries, this will help you reach peak performance in your current role.

Self-discovery is key here—realizing what you're capable of and then growing toward that. *You maximize your job by maximizing your effort.*

Here are some ways you can do that:

1. "Assign" yourself. You no longer need somebody telling you what else to do. Look around and see for yourself where you can step up and help out, even if it's not your team. Then put yourself to work!

Jonathan did exactly that when the record label he just joined was hosting an artist event, which included a banquet. His colleagues who were officially in charge of it had the major aspects covered, but he'd helped with events at his previous company. He knew how stressed his leaders would be when the big evening came. The challenge was always in completing the details before the doors opened. So Jonathan headed to the venue right after work that evening and said, "Put me to work. Want me to help set up the chairs? Finish getting the tables ready? Break down boxes and get them out of the room? What can I do?"

"Yes!" they said. "All of it!"

The next time the company had an event, Jonathan was included as part of the on-site event team. Later, he was asked to join the event-planning committee. And in time, helping plan events became part of his job description.

With choices like this—by attending meetings and events you don't have to, for example—you're acting as a linebacker for your team.

In football, a linebacker literally "backs the front line" of defenders on his team. He has specific assignments, but at the same time, he's on call, ready to dive in and help his teammates with their assignments. This includes going after additional training if you need it. Don't wait for it to be offered to you!

You're the linebacker. Take care of your assignments like a pro *and* be on the lookout to offer hands-on support to the people around you as they're tackling their roles.

2. *Value people.* Relationships precede promotion. Period. Be present with your leaders and teammates. This means join in. Don't eat alone in the breakroom every day. Grab dinner after hours once in a while, attend fun events together, and get to know your coworkers beyond the walls of the office.

This also means saying thank you to those who help you, and giving credit where credit is due. A handwritten note with a gift card is a can't-miss. So is treating an unsung teammate to coffee. Giving a shout-out on social media or commending a coworker in an email to company leadership can also be a great way to lift them up.

Valuing people also means looking for any excuse to celebrate them—job accomplishments, birthdays, or life milestones like weddings or new babies. Celebrating doesn't have to involve an official office party. Some workplaces don't allow these anyway. But no one can stop you from bringing in a little plate of cookies just for that person or a small bouquet of flowers and a card.

By valuing others, you're demonstrating their worth—and proving yours. That's about as promotable as you can get.

3. Speak up. Carole started in financial services right out of college. It's hard to believe, but she's now been in the same role for sixteen years. She's ready for a change and especially ready to move into her dream job. Not too long ago, she sat down with her leaders, and they asked her what her dream job is. With her passion for people, Carole was ready with her answer: "A leader who coaches people in their job."

Her manager suggested that she talk with the human resources department about joining their training group full time, but Carole wants to be a department manager. That's really her goal. She needs to have a clarifying conversation with leadership and tell them, "I really want to lead a team of people instead of HR training. Does this HR role get me there?"

Once she's had that conversation, then she'll know whether she should stay where she is or look to another company.

Maximizing your role includes maximizing your communication. Don't assume your leader knows you want a promotion. Tell them so. Once you've really learned your job, schedule a meeting to share your desire to grow and earn more responsibility. Ask what skills or qualities they would recommend you develop in order for you to reach the goal. Emphasize growth and personal development in the conversation, not a pay raise or a better title. If you're focused on growing, you won't have to worry about the money or the title. They'll follow as you reach your dream.

Your Time Will Come

Though working your way from rung 1 to rung 3 takes time, I'm happy to report that if you're the right person in the right place, doing the right things, *the right time will happen*. Your promotion *will* come.

My dad was the first one to teach me this invaluable lesson.

When I was eight years old, I played soccer in a league for boys ages eight to ten, and I loved everything about it except for the playing time. Or should I say, the *lack* of playing time. Being new to the game definitely kept me on the sidelines. My size, though, was the greater issue. It was, um, *prohibitive*. I had good, raw skills, but I was no bigger than a kindergartner and by far the smallest kid in the league. I'm sure my coach was worried I'd need the paramedics if the ball ever hit me.

I didn't care about any of that. So what if I was a rookie? So what if I was the size of a Chihuahua? I had the determination of a hungry Great Dane. I'd go up against the big kids any day. *Just let me play!*

Nobody likes to sit the bench, but it ripped my little heart out. After a game one day, I couldn't hide it any longer.

I'll never forget that ride home with my dad. I was in the backseat, staring down at my shoes, trying to hold back my emotions. He could tell I was upset by my silence.

"What's wrong, bud?" he asked.

I was so dejected, I couldn't answer at first. Then I burst into tears. Finally, I managed to choke out the words, "I just wanna play!"

My dad eyed me in the rearview mirror and said, "Look, you're the youngest guy and the littlest guy. But in two years, you'll be the oldest guy and you won't be the littlest guy. Your time will come, bud. Keep at it. Just keep working on your game."

His words came true. I got bigger and better, and by the time I was ten, I was a starter and got way more playing time.

That fatherly wisdom has stayed with me. Maybe you need to hear it today too. If you're not yet where you want to be, take my dad's advice: "Keep at it. Your time will come!"

Some things don't change. As an adult, patience *still* doesn't come naturally for me. In the small stuff, like traffic jams, I'm that annoying dude doing U-turns to avoid the standstill. But what *has* changed is my approach in the big things.

A parent understands and expects to wait in line to ride a roller coaster—and they can do it patiently—while their child is just about in fits. Likewise, I've found that embracing the wait gives me staying power. Anything worth having is difficult to obtain. This is true for all of us in relationships, financial investing, and life. Actually *planning* to persist and be patient is what allows us to endure the long haul and appreciate the reward that much more when it comes.

There's no question that we each have to show up and chop away at the work, day after day. But we need the discipline of patience too: persist in the work to get promoted, but then be willing to wait your turn.

Work. And wait.

Wait. And work.

If I can do it, you can do it. Patience can be one of your disciplines even if it's not naturally part of your character.

Whether you're a first-year employee, a seasoned manager, or a dreamer who works for yourself, the secret to getting promoted is to care deeply about what you're doing and take care of business every day—patiently. Focus there, and your career ladder will take care of itself.

Chapter 9 Takeaways

Remember This

If you obsess about the *next* and miss what you need to do
in the *now*, you could ultimately sacrifice the *next*.

You Got This

You earned this role, now own it!

Do This

Review and apply the three actions that will get you promoted.

10

Five Qualities That Bring Promotions to You

*T*hud, thud, thud!

Carolyn Collins was just about to take out the trash when she heard loud knocking on the cafeteria doors. It was early in the morning, and she was alone inside the high school where she worked as a janitor.

She opened the door slowly and saw two students standing nervously in the dark.

"Can we please come in?" asked one of them.

School didn't start for a couple of hours, but she let them in and their story tumbled out. They were homeless and their mom had dropped them off early so they could use the restrooms to get ready for school.

Carolyn's eyes filled with tears as she listened. She told them to sit down at one of the cafeteria tables and went into the kitchen. She returned a moment later with fruit and cereal for the brother and sister. They ate hungrily and soon hurried off to the restroom to get ready for school.

That was all it took. Within two days, Carolyn had purchased essentials like toiletries, underwear, and pencils with her own money, cleaned out a storage closet in the school, and with the administration's blessing, opened a giving closet for any student in need.

That was years ago and she's been doing it ever since. She's "always on the lookout for teens who come to school each day wearing the same clothes, shuffling through the halls with their heads down—a sign that they might be homeless or experiencing other stress. Discreetly, she'll invite them to take a peek in her closet."[46]

What does a high school janitor have to do with getting your dream job? Everything. Yes, it's important to be good at your job. You absolutely have to know what you're doing. But in order to get promoted, you also need to have the right attitude, the right heart. Carolyn wasn't just cleaning and sweeping. She was being herself and went so far above and beyond her role at the school that it changed the lives of people in her community forever. She's the kind of woman who got noticed because she's an extraordinary person. And it's the same heart that gets you noticed for a promotion.

Quality people get promoted because they've paid their dues *and* paid attention. Every day, they're doing their best work and working to be the best version of themselves. That's what getting promoted is really about: what you do (knowing your role, accepting your role, and maximizing your role) and who you are. In chapter 10, we're going to focus on the latter. We're going to talk about how to be the best person for the promotion by becoming the best version of *you*.

Together, your actions and qualities bring the horsepower to your dream. They are career accelerators. With them, there will be no stopping you from reaching the top!

Five Qualities That Get You Promoted

In the progression from where you are to where you're going, leadership expert John Maxwell's Law of Awareness tells us, "You must know yourself to grow yourself."[47] Your mission is to become better today than you were yesterday.

In addition to improving your job skills, focus on becoming the *kind of person* who deserves more responsibility. Here are five specific character qualities that make you promotable:

1. Be Likable

You won't believe how far this simple quality will take you. Technology pioneer and author Tim Sanders asserts that likability is "the key to success" in all of life, including the workplace.[48] He's right! Research overwhelmingly shows that if people like you, they will choose you: buying from you, hiring you, befriending you, marrying you.[49] Likability makes you enormously promotable too. Be the person who others love to be around.

People should smile when they see you at the coffee station or your name on their caller ID. Kindness, warmth, friendliness—these always matter. In the boardroom and the breakroom. A sense of humor helps too. People who naturally laugh at themselves and can laugh at life's quirks project a calm that puts others at ease.

By being likable, you're not trying to pretend to be someone you're not or win a popularity contest. You're simply caring about and enjoying others, like in the Getting Connected stage. Sanders once told a failing radio shock jock, "You will win more friends in the next two months developing a sincere interest in two people than you will ever win in the next two years trying to get two people interested in you."[50]

I can hear some of my introverted friends now: "Does that mean small talk? You know how I feel about small talk!"

You don't love hanging out in the hallways telling stories? No problem. A great way to build likability is to compliment people when you see something about *them* that you like. Though extroverts should make this a habit too, this is an especially good work-around for introverts.

Some of my quieter friends have had colleagues tell them, "Until I got to know you, I was scared of you." The intimidation factor can be strong when you're not super talkative. People don't know how to interpret silence. Coach Pat Summitt tuned in to this dynamic with her players, and her conclusions are very insightful:

> [Over the years] I complimented [my players], but for some reason they didn't register it, whereas they tended to hang on to the critical things I said. Even more important, when they didn't hear my voice at all, they assumed I must be unhappy with them. Which taught me a fundamental lesson: *in the absence of feedback, people will fill in the blanks with the negative. They will assume you don't care about them or don't like them.*[51]

It's sad that it takes so little for others to think that we dislike them! On the other hand, it doesn't take much to convince them that we're in their corner either. Just a quick compliment—"Good job on handling that tough question in the meeting today" or "I like that you're such a people person" or even "Your kids are really cute"—instantly tears down barriers of misunderstanding and endears you to others. So ask simple questions like, "Hey, how was your weekend?" or "How's the project coming?"—and then give your colleague a chance to answer. You're seeing them. You're noticing them. You're communicating that you like them. They will notice and like you right back.

Being likable isn't only for the in-house folks. It's just as critical when you're self-employed. If your connections enjoy you *and* you do great work, that's a can't-miss combination. They'll literally *watch for* opportunities to partner with you. I've known plenty of these corporate decision-makers—the people who handle outsourcing for their companies—and I've heard their stories. Assuming the skill levels are equal, they will pay more to work with someone who is likable over some Grumpy Gus who costs less but complains about the work from start to finish.

Not only will those companies look for chances to choose you, they will also compete to have you on the project! Cameron, a freelance graphic designer, had been in conversations for over a year with one of his favorite new clients—a manufacturer whose work and mission he felt a real kinship with. He'd done a couple of small jobs for them, but the head of the company, Gary, had promised to send a big project Cameron's way someday. It was just a matter of them signing the right partner.

Gary's company had a great reputation, so Cameron believed him, but he also had bills to pay. So he kept hustling and took on other jobs.

Wouldn't you know it? Gary's "perfect project" came along just as Cameron was about to begin a major, months-long project that he'd cleared his schedule for. On the phone, Gary excitedly shared the details. It was absolutely a graphic designer's dream.

Then Cameron asked the big question: "What's your deadline?"

"October 1," Gary replied.

The exact schedule as Cameron's current project.

"I hate to tell you this, Gary, but I have to decline. I've already contracted with another client for this same time frame."

Both men felt disappointed. They'd really wanted to team up.

But then Gary threw out an idea: "What if we moved the schedule? I'm pretty sure we could slot this project for next summer, and from my conversations with our new partner, I think they'd be relieved to have the extra time. Let me talk to them and get back to you."

Gary phoned two days later, and within a week, Cameron was signing a contract for a June delivery on this future job.

Obviously, clients don't always shift their schedules to fit a freelancer's schedule. But it's not as rare as you might imagine. If people like you, they will go out of their way to have you on their team. Whether you're in the office with them or working for yourself, likability makes advancement more likely.

2. Be Coachable

I call coachability the professional version of likability. Someone who is coachable is open to both instruction and correction—the two most common types of job feedback. They're not resistant to input in either form.

Instruction involves learning within the company's system. You may do it better or know a different way, but you need to do it their way. Be a straight-A student in training situations and soak up everything you can. Being coachable means having humility and letting your colleagues and leaders teach you.

The second type of workplace feedback is *correction*: you're doing something that needs to stop or change. Someone who is coachable receives correction and works on their weakness. There are times when correction involves more than making adjustments. Sometimes you have to do a complete 180! Whatever the degree, the coachable one takes the opportunity to learn. I'll give you an example.

A friend of mine had worked for many years for a company where it didn't matter *how* you got the job done—it only mattered that you got it done. Yell at some people? Hurt some feelings? Burn a few bridges? No big deal as long as you achieved your result. Then he took a job with a different company who cared deeply about how the work got done. When he walked into his annual review at the end of his first year, his leader said, "Listen, I don't care how good you are at your job. If you don't stop running over people, you're out." He was stunned, but he got the message and immediately began making changes.

Being coachable is probably the number one indicator of promotability, which makes sense when you think about it. Getting promoted means learning new skills, new processes—and making mistakes you've never made before. You will need both instruction and correction on the path ahead.

I'm sure some of you, at the mention of *correction* (which should mean constructive criticism) are replaying the ugly scenarios you've endured that weren't constructive.

Those times when you were yelled at instead of talked to.

Blamed and belittled, not shown the way.

Humiliated, not helped.

I've been there too, and I can think of examples instantly. It's almost impossible to forget those hot-seat experiences where correction was handled so badly. Criticism can be poorly received for a lot of reasons, like a terrible delivery or a toxic messenger. It's not always a matter of being uncoachable.

Let me give you some tools for sifting the gold from the dirt so you can win the *now* in this area.

From Correction to Promotion

I'm highlighting this, not only due to the direct connection between "correctability" and promotability, but because correction (and sometimes instruction too) is often terribly mishandled by the ones we're working so hard for.

The thing is, whether it's communicated well or not, it's up to us to respond well. I'll give you a few ways that have helped me in tough situations.

Let's say that our "corrector" is more typical—an inexperienced or awkward communicator, not a complete jerk. These conversations still hurt. They may not leave a scar, but they cause plenty of emotional indigestion.

Our lizard brain is quick to misunderstand, misinterpret, and misuse what we've been told. It immediately goes to defense mode, wanting to shut down or fight back. What can we do to counteract our instincts?

Give yourself ninety seconds before you say a word. The Bible says, "It is never fun to be corrected. In fact, at the time it is always painful."[52] Isn't that the truth? Even if it's done with the glove of a dove (which it often isn't), criticism and instruction can still sting. Instantly, it feels personal. We feel exposed, vulnerable. In those moments, give your lizard brain the ninety seconds it needs to gather itself and get past the point of impact. Then you'll be better prepared to filter the words and find the intended message. Filtering is the way to respond to any type of correction.

Sift the instruction through the sieve of humility and truth. We all know some leaders are better at correction than others. And we've probably all had a leader or two who were toxic. When I'm being corrected, I start with: *Are they for me?*

If they are, I try to hear the person out and give them some grace even if they don't say things the right way. If the corrector is toxic, then your filter has to be twofold: *This isn't really about me* and *Find the nugget of truth.*

Hurting people hurt people. Don't take their words personally. Reminding yourself of that can help you feel less of a sting. So don't get hung up on the messenger. Instead, explore the message: *What is the thing they want corrected?* Filter it on your own terms: *What do I need to learn? What should I correct?* There's always something you can get out of it.

Filter the corrector's intent so you can focus on the work. If you're still troubled by the correction, then pass it through a second filter. Besides looking for what you can learn, try to filter the corrector's intent. In the big picture, what are they really trying to accomplish?

A scholarship athlete in his freshman year of college once asked me what to do about his coach, who was consistently ripping him in practices. The coach would yell at Micah in front of the entire team, acting like he was the drill instructor at a boot camp.

Micah was shocked the first time it happened. He thought maybe it was a fluke. But it was continuing to happen, and he was reeling.

"I'm thinking of transferring to another school," he confided. The yelling felt really personal to him because he was a guy with a great attitude. Plus, his high school coaches hadn't been shouters.

Some of the older players had assured him, "Coach Al does that to everybody." And he'd seen that for himself: the other guys got hounded too; it wasn't just Micah. Their coach was coaching everybody (although probably louder than was necessary). If the leader does it to everybody, then you're not being singled out. You can take it if you're not the only one.

So Micah's second filter had to be: *What is Coach's intent? Is he trying to humiliate me? Or is he trying to make me better?*

Unless you're dealing with an abuser or someone who is unstable, your critic is not out to ruin you. They're usually attempting to correct something that's off so you can get better. With this secondary filter, Micah could see: "Coach Al is trying to prepare me for the pros."

Focus on what your critic is up to beyond the words or the volume. Good leaders are in it with you, working to help you. They're pointing out something that you aren't seeing in order to grow you and improve you. If this person were trying to fire you or get rid of you, that would be a whole different conversation.

Once Micah realized this was his coach's way of teaming up with him, he could go back in and face the criticism. He would never love the yelling, but he didn't need to leave the program either. His goal of going pro was within reach, and Coach Al was intent on helping him get there.

Handling the wounds correctly makes a difference. Once you've gotten the diagnosis and you understand the doctor's intent, you can apply the medicine and get back to work. You may remember the wound for a very long time, but it will heal. In time you will no longer feel the pain. Especially when the promotion happens.

By staying coachable, we win the moment *and* we prove that we're in the game and ready for more.

3. Be Reliable

You build trust over time by being reliable. This is the third character trait that gets you promoted.

In the previous chapter, we saw how Andrea stepped it up for her company during the months of the pandemic. She worked extra hours, took on extra duties, covered the details to keep the team from dropping the ball. She also made sure she delivered on her promises.

How reliable are you? What's your answer to questions like these?

- Can people trust me?
- Do I do a good job with more on my plate?
- When my name is on a project, does my team immediately know it's in good hands?

Being reliable includes being a watchdog. Do you keep watch over your responsibilities so you can sound an alert if your team or company is heading toward an iceberg? When your coworkers and leaders know you're looking out for them, they can settle in and do *their* job.

In her first year with a new company, Meredith made the mistake of not telling her supervisor, Casey, that one phase of a project was going off the rails. A vendor was running behind and wouldn't be able to deliver their piece until a week later.

The vendor offered a discount for the inconvenience, and Meredith approved the schedule change, pleased that she could save her boss the hassle and save the company a little cash. What she didn't anticipate was that Casey's boss, the CEO, would ask *Casey* about the status. Because Casey hadn't been told about the altered schedule, she mistakenly assured her leader that everything was running on time.

The next day, Casey asked Meredith for an update. Casey wasn't happy to be hearing the news after the fact. Yet she also understood that her new hire was trying to be proactive, not deceptive. Meredith apologized, sorry that she had let her leader down. The two of them talked it out, and Casey gave Meredith some advice that she has heeded ever since with each of her leaders: *No surprises.*

"Don't let me be blindsided," Casey said. "Warn me when something starts to slip through the cracks." She added, "You won't ever be in trouble for telling me. Things go wrong all the time in this business. But make sure I know about it so we can figure out a different plan of attack."

In that experience, Meredith exhibited another trust builder: being quick to fix anything you break. This is one of the most attractive qualities in the world! Be responsive to right your wrongs on the job and to mend fences with others. When you've dropped the ball or forgotten something or didn't handle things right, own it. Apologize. Make amends and do better next time. No excuses.

Your coworkers and leaders must be able to count on you with *all the things*: Communication. Deadlines. Tasks. Meeting preparation. (That last category is an often overlooked indicator of reliability, so take the time to prepare for every meeting you're invited to!)

And last but not least, to be reliable, take steps to be emotionally healthy. Reliability in this regard can't be overestimated.

Pat Summitt was the first basketball coach in NCAA history (male or female) to reach 1,000 wins. When she retired in 2012, not only was she the winningest college basketball coach of all time, but her teams had also won more national championships than any coach except UCLA's John Wooden. As you'd expect, she had team dynamics on the mind practically every day of her career. In her last book before her untimely death, she offered this about the need to be emotionally reliable:

> [Others] only follow you if they find you consistently credible. . . . If teammates find you the least bit inconsistent, moody, unpredictable, indecisive, or emotionally unreliable, then they balk and the whole team is destabilized. . . . If there is a single ingredient in leadership, it's emotional maturity.[53]

You may not be a designated leader in your workplace yet, but your teammates still need for you to be a stabilizing force. Your day-to-day steadiness in your demeanor, in your treatment of people, and in your approach to problem solving helps everybody stay on course and deliver their best. It also gets you noticed by your leaders.

4. Be Adaptable

Being adaptable makes you not only the ultimate team player but eventually gets you promoted to team captain. Adaptability is one of the most important qualities for managers. To be able to manage change yourself and within a team is a true mark of leadership.

Think of the last time you were presented with a new technology or process in your job. How did you react? Did you cross your arms and only halflisten? Did you keep interrupting with reasons it wouldn't work? Or did you say, "Yeah, it's time. I'm going to embrace it and do my part to support the effort"?

Though change is often needed, I don't know too many people who love it. Some personality types thrive on the adrenaline, but for most of us, transitions mean yet another bout with Fear, Doubt, or Pride.

Not knowing how things will work out is really scary. But remember: when your whole team is facing a transition at work, nobody really knows the best path *for sure*. If you're willing to embrace the transition, and collaborate with others who are doing the same, then you're likely in store for a good outcome.

In a changing environment, your leader's plate is already full. That person has to deal with the corporate and team demands, as well as making the transition themselves. They need to know that when a forced change is thrown at you, you can handle it. You'll catch the ball and run with it, adapting as needed.

The adaptable person can move between these different spaces mentally and emotionally without melting down: "You need me to totally change gears? Open up a new district office? Oversee this massive project? Take on more work after the layoffs? Okay. I haven't done it before, but I can learn. We'll figure it out as we go."

The ability to adapt starts with that kind of spirit—a willingness to do whatever it takes. It's a can-do outlook, a will-do mentality, a collaborative approach, and a rugged determination to get busy and deliver your very best.

If adaptability doesn't come naturally to you, build up that muscle before you need to flex it. Here are some ways to do that:

Force some changes on yourself. Bestselling author Brené Brown has said, "We can choose courage or we can choose comfort, but we can't have both."[54] In your work, your relationships, your routines—wherever you tend to be inflexible—stir things up. Get out of your comfort zone by learning a new skill or volunteering for an assignment you wouldn't normally choose. Or challenge yourself to figure out a different solution to an old problem. The better you get at creative solutions, the more confident you'll be when change comes.

Get to the heart. Ever notice how easy it is to go to the worst-case scenario when uncertainty strikes? Besides taking your fear to court with the three-part process we discussed in chapter 7, explore: What is it about change that you don't like? What Fear or Doubt does it spark? Why do you resist it? Also, analyze what causes it to feel so uncomfortable for you. Once we understand these things, it opens the floodgates to new ways of thinking.

Interview your coworkers. Watch for who navigates change well and learn how they handle their toughest challenges. Get their tips for embracing change—before any change comes.

Start viewing your mistakes through a different lens. Adaptable people aren't deterred by failure. They know that mastering anything new—a hobby, sport, or skill—means you face-plant once in a while. Consider mistakes your practice runs rather than viewing them as wins or losses. Casting them in that light will help you look at them differently.

And, once you've learned from your mistakes, get used to dropping them and leaving them behind for good. Replaying them keeps you tied to the past. To be adaptable, you have to keep a cool head. Anytime you mess up, reset. Practice getting back up quickly. Studies have shown that those who do experience more success than people who dwell on their mistakes. Staying light on your feet lets you pivot. The quicker you learn to recover now, the better you'll be when the clock is running and the pressure's on.

5. Be Honorable

The last quality that makes you promotable is being honorable. This takes different forms, from having manners to acting with integrity. It also means treating people with the respect and dignity you want to be treated with.

You exhibit this quality in spades in three common on-the-job scenarios:

- when you and a colleague disagree
- when you're responsible for correcting someone
- when you're among toxic or dysfunctional people

Very quickly, let's run through each of these and consider what an honorable approach looks like.

When you and a colleague disagree: In any setting where money, reputation, and livelihood are at stake, some conflict is inevitable. And when people care deeply about the work, the intensity of a disagreement can throw you. Emotions can get heated—fast. Being honorable means keeping a cool head, an open mind, and a humble heart, wanting a win for both sides.

Disagreements don't have to become arguments. At least not for you. Your goals are respectful dialogue and fair compromise. Others may resort to name-calling or finger-pointing or pouting. Instead, I want you to learn conflict-resolution techniques and boundaries and practice role-playing those emotionally charged conversations with a friend beforehand.

Your training will kick in when the sparks start to fly. You can always ultimately agree to disagree, but treating everyone with dignity gives you good standing with the people in your midst. And remember your fail-safe: get some space from the situation if you or anyone else is starting to get upset. Just a few minutes or a night of sleep for everyone to cool off can do wonders for bringing people back together.

When you're responsible for correction: When I have to correct someone, whether it's one of my kids or someone I work with, I often recall my drama teacher's approach when she confronted me about coming to rehearsal without knowing my lines. Mrs. Bryant delivered the correction that day in very positive ways: She began with her belief in me. She kept to the facts. She kept her voice calm. She kept it short and got straight to the point—and then we all went back to work.

I also really appreciate that she corrected me privately. Sure, my castmates were standing around nearby, but she kept her voice down and turned her back to them so only I could hear. I was already embarrassed by my behavior and having to be corrected at all. She let me save face in front of my peers, which allowed me to get the message despite my emotions.

I respected her in that moment—and still do—for treating *me* with respect. As tough as it is to receive correction, giving it is no cakewalk either. Especially if you care to do it well.

I legitimately disappointed my favorite teacher that day. She had expectations of me, which she called out. At the same time, she honored me by remembering that I had feelings too. Her example showed me that I can honor others by correcting them with regard and respect.

When you're among toxic or dysfunctional people: Being honorable includes rising above the dysfunction in your workplace. Even great companies will have a rotten egg or two among them. It could be a boss, a coworker, or an entire department of gossips and schemers. You don't need a psychology degree to know to stay as far away from these folks as you can. They may not be very toxic to you because you don't play their games. But you can't risk becoming associated with them. Your coworkers—especially leaders—pay attention to who you hang with, and they assume that birds of a feather flock together. They're not going to promote you if they suspect that you're okay with the backbiting, baiting, or bullying of that crowd.

For those times when you do have to work with toxic people to get your job done, keep to the high road. Don't lower yourself to their tactics. You always have an option: silence over insults, positivity over negativity, perspective over blame. Be a light. Set a quiet example. You'll stay promotable.

Grow to Go

Getting promoted involves consistency *and* completion. The Navy SEALs approach their work with a "complete the mission" mindset, and so should we. Finish your mission by *becoming* your best, not just *doing* your best.

To rise up the company ladder, you must do all that you're called to do—and be all that you're called to be. The two are inseparable.

So keep asking yourself: *Where else can I grow?* And ask a trusted friend at work to give you some honest input on where you're doing well and where you can improve. Then complete your mission by continually becoming the best version of yourself. Make sure you're expanding your efforts and adding to your character every single day.

With time, a promotion will find you. You can't always predict the exact moment, but when the time comes to throw your hat in the ring, you can rest assured you've done the work necessary to earn your spot.

You've won the *now*.

You're ready for the *next*.

Remember This

You will get promoted when you do your best work
and work to be the best version of you!

You Got This

You are the only person who can put a lid on you.

Do This

Review the five qualities and evaluate how much
you can develop those in your work.

STAGE 6

Get Your Dream Job

11

How to Tell the Difference Between the Dream and a Mirage

I'm such a fool! she thought.

Rachel had taken her dream job with her dream company just three months before. The first week was fantastic. Her job description was her sweet spot to a T. She was passionate about the mission of the company. She'd had lunch with her new coworkers and was enjoying getting to know them. She liked the view from her office windows. Even the commute was short!

And then it all slowly began unraveling.

At first she thought she'd just misunderstood what her new boss had said. *He couldn't possibly have meant that the mission of the company was just lip service.* Then she started seeing the quick eye rolls and catching snide comments muttered quietly behind closed doors. *No, no, they don't mean any harm. They're just having a hard day.* Then the kicker came. She was told there weren't resources available to do what she'd been hired to do. They really needed her to do this other job—and it was work that sucked the life right out of her.

By six weeks in, Rachel was genuinely concerned, and by twelve weeks in, she knew she'd made a terrible mistake. It was the worst combination of deceit and dysfunction. Her leader was a complete fake who turned out to be a complete jerk. This wasn't anything close to her dream job, and it definitely wasn't her dream company. She was beside herself.

Dream Job or Mirage?

Everything till now has been about the climb. Hustle, hustle, hustle. You've worked your tail off through all the ups and downs so you could finally be able to seek—and find—your dream job. Now you have an offer in hand for the kind of work you've been created to do. But before you accept this fantastic new opportunity, you need to make sure it's truly your dream and not a mirage.

Here's the reality: it's very possible that you'll receive multiple job offers at this stage of the game because employers see something special in you. They see your focus, your drive, your intentionality, how well you've prepared. Who wouldn't want someone like you on their team?

But I want you to be selective. You may be tempted to run headlong into the first dreamy-looking option you see, like the cartoon character who thinks he's swan-diving into an oasis in the desert, only to end up face-planted in the sand. Instead, before you say yes to what looks like a dream, step back and assess each job carefully.

You have to make sure this is real.

Four Filters

Everybody is susceptible to mirages at Stage 6, Get Your Dream Job. But instead of an optical illusion, we're duped by an opportunity illusion. And it's very easy to do.

Where do people go wrong? What entices us into a mirage rather than our dream job? Things like pay and perks (the *compensation temptation*) or prestige (the *comparison temptation*), where we're chasing a title or a sexy brand. These options speak to what pays good, feels good, and looks good to everybody else.

Those are no-brainers, right? Why not say yes?

It's a no-brainer until you remember what you're after.

In some ways, getting the dream job is like choosing who you're going to marry: you want the complete package. It's not enough to think someone is cute or for them to make a good income. You need to be compatible, to hold similar values. So be picky and hold out until you find the job that offers these four factors *combined* in one opportunity:

- the right work
- the right pay
- the right environment
- the right timing

You want all four lining up. That's the *career grand slam* right there.

Any one of these things can make a job look better than it really is. The job you've been offered might be a match in three of these four areas. But if one of them isn't lining up, keep looking. It's not the job for you.

Because not every option is the right opportunity, let's look at how to apply these four filters to make sure you choose not just what's better but the absolute best for you.

Filter #1: The Right Work

This is the right *role*.

Fancy job titles and vague job descriptions can be a mirage. Stay in your unique role. That's been the dream all along.

Go back to your sweet spot. (Yes, again!) It's the right work for you if . . .

- You're using your top talents and best qualities for most of your day (at least three-quarters of your time).
- You have high emotion and devotion for the work. Time disappears. It often doesn't feel like work.
- It creates results that move your heart and fulfill your deepest desires.

If all that's true from what you can tell from your interviews and research, then check it against the purpose statement you wrote in chapter 2. Your purpose statement is the mold. Does this job fit your mold?

I love watching car restorations on TV. You name the show and I've not only seen it, but I've probably watched every episode. One of the dramatic moments is when the restorers have to take a part from another old car to complete the work. Then comes the moment of truth. They hold it over where it should go. They attach it. Does it fit?

One way you'll know if the position fits is if it frees you to focus on the "artistry" of your work. Every job requires technical skills. But the dream should allow you to expand your creativity as well. (Stick with me. This is true for everyone, not only creative types.)

Think about a famous music artist you follow. They've long since learned the fundamentals of musicianship, stage performance, and songwriting. But once they got the album deal, they could explore their craft in a way they'd never had a chance to do.

If you visited with them today and asked, "So, are you done now with music since you've written some hits for others and recorded an album?" . . . take one guess at what they'd say.

"No way, man! My best songs are yet to be written."

Your dream job will free you up to do the best work of your life because you're in your sweet spot—with the ease, efficiency, and expertise that comes with doing what you were born to do.

When it's the right job, there's a sacredness to your work. What you do will have an artistic flair, a beauty, a *next level* to it that others notice. They'll see it in the way you serve customers, how you innovate when problems come up, and the extra care and effort you put in.

One of my friends knew he'd found the best mechanic in town when he walked in to pick up his car after an engine repair and the mechanic was wiping the engine clean by hand. To top it off, the mechanic, Lance (who also owned the tiny shop), had kept the parts he'd replaced so he could show my friend what the problem was.

Lance's shop was one of two small units in a metal building on the outskirts of town. The shop had room for only three cars at a time, and he and his brother, Mike, did all the work themselves. It was nothing fancy, but the shop was orderly. The prices were fair. Lance treated his customers with integrity and kept his promises. And the shop was never without customers because others had found Lance too.

My buddy estimates that he's referred at least a dozen of his friends to Lance. This was years ago, and Lance's shop is not only thriving, but they've also moved to a roomier location.

This is what I mean. People don't think of mechanics as being artists, except for the guys doing the paint job or restoring cars. But the engine guy? The one fixing your brakes or replacing your starter? Isn't that stuff about nuts and bolts?

The artistry is in the work, but it's reflecting the person's heart. A machinist, a mechanic, an electrician, a fireman, a coach, a farmer, a store manager can bring a creative flair to their job just as readily as a designer or a photographer. Their heart shows in their problem-solving, their people skills, their expertise, their approach, mindset, and attitude. You'll see the love, not the labor.

Filter #2: The Right Pay

Will and his wife aren't expecting a baby yet, but they hope to be within the next year or so. With that possibility in mind, Will is concerned about taking a $13,000 pay cut to pursue his dream job as a career counselor for college students. He can see some very real perks to the switch, despite the decrease in pay. Besides doing what he loves, he'd eventually make more money than he is in his current job. It would also give him and his wife an excuse to relocate and be around friends and family—a blessing if they do have a baby.

Then again, he has an offer for an $8,000 pay raise elsewhere. It would be a good job, but his heart is with the job that would pay him less. How important is the pay? Will following his heart cause his family to struggle?

Compensation can be extremely misleading. A lot of people want to filter the dream through the lens of higher pay alone. This is the one I see most people taking a job for—and getting it wrong. Sometimes pay points you to your dream job, but not always. And certainly not as the sole factor.

Dollar signs have this magnetic effect on us that's hard to resist—at least they do until you're in a job you can't stand. Then you're saying, "I'd give anything to be doing something I love."

Making more won't make you happier, folks! No matter how much you're being paid, you'll dread each day if this job doesn't pass the other three filters. If the reason you're attracted to a job is pay alone, it's not the dream job. You think I'm crazy? Let's check out the data!

Money doesn't buy you happiness. That's what researchers at Princeton's Woodrow Wilson School concluded after analyzing the responses of 450,000 US residents to a Gallup-Healthways poll. At that time, $75,000 a year was the magic number, the "happy" salary. The lower people's income fell beneath that, the less happy they were when they woke up in the morning, but beyond this figure, workers didn't report any further happiness when the alarm clock went off.[55]

Nowhere in the various lists of things people regret on their deathbeds is "I wish I'd made more money." People think about impact, relationships, and missed experiences in their final days, not their bank accounts.

Your dream job should never be about money; *it should always be about meaning*.

Keep the pay in its place—don't let it overly discourage or overly encourage your dream. I say that because you can always make more if you're currently making less, but you don't always have the dream job staring you in the face.

Will and his wife don't know how long it might take them to get pregnant, or if they'll be able to at all. Having been down this long and winding path with my own wife, I sometimes have to remind people that there are no guarantees. But let's assume Will and his wife do get pregnant in the next year. We're still talking many months before they bring their new baby home. And with the support of family close by, they may have additional (and free!) childcare options they wouldn't have if they stayed put. So a decrease in pay right now isn't nearly the risk that it feels like.

No matter what Will brings in at the moment, he and his wife can make adjustments and figure out the money piece as their life unfolds. They have time to plan the finances and work the plan. And they don't know how quickly Will might get promoted. He can always take on a side job—and his wife can keep working too. In this way, the young couple can produce the "right pay." But Will shouldn't keep the dream waiting.

What's Enough for You?

The right pay isn't a number. Would we all take a $20,000 bump in our salary? Sure. But you don't tie the dream job to a dollar figure.

I see teachers working around their salary limits all the time. I wish they didn't have to, but they represent what's possible. Let's look at some stats to paint the picture.

According to the National Education Association, experienced public high school teachers in the US have an average salary of $62,000 per year, while starting teachers average $45,000 or less.[56] A recent Economic Policy Institute report indicates that teachers are paid only 80 percent of what their equals (individuals with similar experience and education) in other professions make.[57]

Clearly, they aren't in it for the money. Most chose teaching because they're invested in helping kids' dreams come true. They're the ultimate dream givers.

The teachers I talk to have . . . *enough*. So does everybody else who's working their dream job. What do I mean by that? If you're in your sweet spot, you'll make enough, whatever "enough" is for you.

Though teachers almost everywhere are underpaid, more of them become "everyday millionaires" than nearly any other profession. Ramsey Solutions did a national study of 10,000 millionaires in 2018, and after accountants and engineers (fields that are known for high incomes), teachers were the third most-likely group to have saved up seven figures. They were more likely to be millionaires than lawyers, doctors, and corporate executives. In fact, one-third of all the millionaires in the study never made $100,000 in any year of their career. I would venture that last stat is true of virtually every millionaire teacher they talked to.

What does that tell us? Your income doesn't determine the size of your bank account—your mindset and behavior do. Teachers know up front that their pay will be limited. So they budget and plan accordingly. They sacrifice, learning to live on less. They save and invest wisely, letting compound growth do for their future what a salary never could. They take on extra jobs. They make it work because they love their work.

In the national millionaire study, Ramsey Solutions also discovered that 96 percent of millionaires enjoyed what they did for a career and 64 percent loved their jobs. Obviously you do need to make enough to pay your bills and work toward your financial goals, like retirement. But beyond that, people who love what they do will simplify their lifestyle to keep doing what they love. As a result, they end up stronger not just financially but emotionally.

Now, I realize that life sometimes puts us in a season where we simply can't take on two jobs or cut back on our expenses to make the leap to the dream. Maybe you're a single parent with little ones, or you're caring for an elderly parent when you're not at work. In circumstances like these, I encourage you to explore the range of options within your unique role where you can make more money *in that one job* and still be in your sweet spot.

For example, as a teacher, what about taking a college or university position? Or moving into the corporate sector with your teaching skills? None of these have to be permanent stops, but you'd still be in your sweet spot. Don't limit your thinking to what you've always done. Do your homework too. As you research, listen for, and watch for other possibilities, you'll almost inevitably run across something you've been overlooking.

No matter what, don't let money be your driving force. Be driven by love of the work and the results. Most of the time, you can flex financially to make the dream work.

Filter #3: The Right Environment

"I'm tired of being treated like I don't matter."

I could hear the weariness in Vicky's voice. For years she'd been in the public school system, working with special-ed students, but she'd also been a mentor for other teachers. She was worn out, though, and feeling burned out.

"I'm open to a different career option," she told me. "I just don't have a lot of confidence in myself and my skills. I'm wondering how I overcome that hurdle."

When I asked Vicky to list the top skills that made her a great special-ed teacher, she named five or six big ones right off. No hesitation. Among those skills: writing curriculum and breaking big concepts into small, learnable chunks. She ended her list with a little summary of herself: "I'm a chameleon of sorts and a people person. I like reaching out to faculty members and working with them one-on-one. I'm able to give up what I do to blend into other people's classrooms. That's the best part of my job, helping others succeed and do things they didn't think they could do."

With such an incredible skill set, honed over nearly twenty years in a difficult environment, that role of hers could fit in a lot of places. She just couldn't see it in the moment. For Vicky, it won't matter whether she's in a classroom, a boardroom, or at a training center. She'll be bringing that absolute arsenal of talents with her wherever she goes.

By the end of our call, she was chuckling at how well-suited she was for living the dream someplace else. "I'm not gonna lie! I'm feelin' pretty good right about now!" she said.

I loved hearing her laughter. After seventeen years in a school system, Vicky had developed blinders. She thought that was the only setting she could thrive in. But once she took off the blinders and got a full view of the scenery around her, she had an entire world of possibilities.

Many of us get stuck in a mental and emotional spin cycle: *Oh my gosh, I've been doing this for so long, can I even function outside of this workplace, this field?* Sure you can!

Anytime you wonder, *What's going on? I'm doing what I love, but I'm miserable!* you're in the right role but the wrong place. You can be in the center of your sweet spot and fail to thrive because of your environment. If this is what you're experiencing, now is a good time to take my free quiz Should I Quit My Job? at https://www.ramseysolutions.com/career -advice/should-i-quit-my-job-quiz.. It will help you determine whether or not you're in both the right role and the right place. You may not need to change careers—you might just need to change locations.

This is why you must do "environmental testing" throughout your career. You have to keep your radar up for the *best* place for you. It's so easy to settle for a better environment at this stage because the one you're in is so bad that *anything* would be better. But this is your dream job we're talking about. Make sure you're not just running from where you are but that you're drawn to this new place. Chase the dream job into the very best setting for you.

What to Look For

When you were getting started in Stage 4, you were seeking a good environment, but the workplace wasn't as big of a concern. You knew you were going to move on.

In your dream job, the environment—the people, the culture, and the mission—becomes a nonnegotiable. It's the difference between renting a house and building your dream home.

With the rental, you're looking for a nice place that takes care of your needs. Is it clean? Decent neighborhood? Does it have enough bedrooms and bathrooms for us to get by? Is it within our budget? Once you've toured it and had your basic questions answered, that's all you need to know. It might be a ten-minute decision because it's not permanent.

Building your dream home? That's a months-long process that involves very detailed planning before the first shovel goes into the ground. It often takes a year or two from start to finish—and that's after you decide on the right location. You're setting down roots. It's a whole different deal.

Working for a name-brand company or organization in your field can be as much of a mirage as a high salary. It may not actually be what you think you want. So don't make assumptions about a place because of the hype. You're seeking a place where you can "live long and prosper" versus have bragging rights with your friends and family.

The right environment features these three elements:

1. A growth environment. Your dream job needs to be in a growth environment. Be sure you'll be where you can keep growing. Is there a clear path forward for you? There may only be a few titles above yours, but is there room for expansion for you? Is this a place that will encourage growth and allow you to increase your expertise and influence? Remember, you'll not only be living the dream there, but you'll also be building a career that you can grow in for the rest of your life. This is where I am now. I'm in my dream job, but I'm doing it in the right environment at Ramsey Solutions because I know I'm building a platform and business model that will outlive me.

2. A missional environment. It's not enough to appreciate or like what a company or organization does. Your dream job needs to have a mission you *love*. In fact, it should feel like an extension of your own. The product they deliver or the service they provide has to match your passion and mission. But you also want to make sure their approach to business aligns with yours.

Do they care about excellence as much as you do? Do they share your same priorities regarding customers or their treatment of team members? Are they fiscally responsible? Do they care about the community they're in and causes that matter deeply to you? Don't just stick your finger in the air and ask, "Does this feel good?" You need to find out if there's real alignment. Do you connect to their values to your core?

3. A healthy environment. The third element you're looking for in the right environment is overall health. If your workplace is toxic, it will feel like you're in a battle every single day.

Besides diving deeper into the healthy culture research I recommended in chapter 8 (page 148), pay attention to the following markers:

- *Leadership and the majority of team members are crusaders of the mission.* They're engaged, aware, enthusiastic, unified, and working toward the same vision. Marcus Buckingham (one of my heroes and one of the minds behind the StrengthsFinder movement) has learned that people leave their managers, not their companies. What kind of reputation does the leadership have? The employees? Do you know someone who works there, or a friend of a friend you can talk to? Good leadership draws good employees, and good employees become good teams.

- *The company takes steps to avoid toxicity.* How they deal with toxic or difficult people will tell you what you need to know. Are difficult people promoted? Is gossip rampant? Do the leaders have toxic tendencies? Toxic leaders have their heads in the sand. They either don't recognize the jerk (whether the jerk is them or someone else), or they don't care. A great culture develops, promotes, encourages, and empowers healthy employees. How long do people stay? Do they only like it there, or do they love it? These are things to explore as you're considering your options.

- *The team is a group of high-caliber people who challenge one another to be better.* The Proximity Principle that was so important as you were getting connected remains incredibly essential now. You need to be around other high achievers who will push you and make you better. These are people who care about the team around them, not just themselves—and people who will welcome a challenge from you rather than try to shut you down or silence you.

Filter #4: The Right Timing

If everything else is right, the right time reveals itself. You won't have to force it.

Billy Donovan learned this firsthand. After winning two national championships as the head coach for the University of Florida, he accepted a position as head coach for the NBA's Orlando Magic. It was more prestige, more money, more pressure—more everything. And within twenty-four hours of announcing his decision, he knew he'd made a mistake. His children were young, and he knew it was going to be too much. After several days of negotiations, the Magic released him from his contract and Billy returned to the University of Florida.

Eight seasons later, once his kids were older, he was offered another opportunity to be a coach in the NBA—this time as head coach for the Oklahoma City Thunder. He took it because he knew it was right for everyone.

A dream job is going to work not just for you but for your family too. If the price is too high for the people you love, it's not the right time.

- For Melanie to take the dream job she'd been offered, she would be moving her daughter just before the girl's senior year of high school.
- Juan's dream job would let him work from home on Fridays, but he'd be on the road three to four days a week—after his wife had just delivered twins.
- Seth and Sherry's son was autistic. They had struggled for years to find the right school for him and had finally found

one that was delivering great results. But Sherry's dream job meant relocating.

- As much as she loved a challenge, Kellie didn't have peace about switching to a higher-stress job where she'd be working sixty hours a week. Not right then, when her mother was in the late stages of dementia with no other family nearby.

When is the right time to step into your dream job? When the first three filters deliver a yes and no pressing personal or family matters are preventing it. Sometimes taking the dream job will create a hardship for you, or someone you love, that isn't worth it. Only you can make that call. Your heart will tell you. Listen to it and trust it, whatever it says.

If all four filters have been applied and it's clear you should step into your dream job, don't put it off! Don't go after your dreams later. You'll have excuses later too, and the older you get, the more complex your life usually becomes.

When it's the right thing all the way around, it'll be the right time.

Stay Focused

Let me prepare you for something that is almost sure to happen if you've approached your work the way we've discussed in this book. People will start seeing your output and they'll want to promote you. Be careful, though, because they might promote you right out of your dream job.

I get so many calls from people who were enticed away by better pay or status, but they can't stand their new job. The results and the work don't fire them up. They call and ask what any of us would ask: "Should I go back to what I was doing?"

The answer is to be clear on what your *next* is. What is it you really want? It's not enough that a fun, new opportunity just landed in your lap. It must align with where you're going.

This is why we get clear again and again—and try to stay clear at every stage—so that we don't go after something sparkly that catches our eye but won't fill up our hearts. You may have the talent and enjoy the work, but if it's not on mission, then it's not for you.

I realize the risk involved: "What if I turn down the promotion because it isn't right for me? Will they overlook me next time?" First of all, we don't know. Secondly, it doesn't really matter. If it's a mirage, you'll be miserable. You want to stay with the dream you've been chasing.

Reaching the Dream

As you keep rising through the ranks, you'll eventually land your dream job—and let me tell you, that's an incredible feeling.

When you finally say yes to the dream, take the time to celebrate. Milestones deserve their moment in the sun. Whatever's next can wait.

I get irritated when I hear a coach say after winning a championship, "I'll be back in the office watching film tomorrow." *No, dude, reflect on the journey, savor the victory, and take a vacation to enjoy!*

Setting aside time to say, "Woo-hoo! We did it!" with your loved ones is incredibly important. It's a time to honor your family, your friends, and the journey itself. If you don't celebrate it, you're missing the beauty of the journey.

Sir Edmund Hillary, the great mountain climber who was the first to summit Everest, called himself "a lucky man," saying, "I have had a dream and it has come true, and that is not a thing that happens often to men."[58]

He was right—it doesn't often happen. That's why it's worth marking. It wasn't luck for Hillary, and it won't be a matter of luck for you. Hillary's quest had begun fourteen years earlier, when he'd reached his first big summit at age twenty. From that point on, he was doing the work that made *this* dream—his Everest—possible. That's what you've been doing too. And by reaching your goal and getting your dream job, *you* will achieve what few people ever do.

It's as big an accomplishment as you think it is, so acknowledge it in a way you'll never forget.

Right now I can't help but picture the party Stacy and I had at my best friend's house in October of 2017 to celebrate the SiriusXM radio launch. The entire team was there. She and I gave each person a gift, but I also went around the room one by one and thanked each person specifically.

Be sure to pause to reflect and reminisce privately as well. It's the after-party effect, where you've had such a great celebration with the people you love most, to acknowledge the accomplishment and a dream come true, but then you're by yourself, kicking one of the balloons gently in the air and appreciating the experience of getting there.

When you remember the pain, the rejection, and the frustration, it becomes obvious: this was indeed a journey to a new frontier! A mountain conquered! You remember the cramps, the blisters, the cold, the heat, the doubts and fears, and delays. But you also recall that irreplaceable moment when you crested the hill, crossed the finish, and planted your flag at the top.

It's so sweet because it was so hard. In a few days, you can return to the dream. For now, savor it.

Chapter 11 Takeaways

Remember This
Make sure the dream job is not a mirage.

You Got This
You are special—hold out for a special opportunity.

Do This
Review and vet your current opportunity according
to the four filters in this chapter.

12

How to Keep the Dream from Becoming a Nightmare

Talk about the right guy at the right time. My buddy Nick is so smart, so unbelievably talented, that while still in his twenties, he was catapulted into the top role of the tech company he'd joined. Anytime his name was mentioned, even among those of us who were his friends, it was with a certain amount of awe. He was the Kobe Bryant of his industry, a professional prodigy who was as confident as he was talented and laser-focused on winning big.

In Nick's first years as CEO, the company saw stratospheric growth. He brought fresh ideas for product and marketing, and as the company flourished, so did Nick. Functioning completely in his sweet spot, he had everything a guy could want: a sterling reputation, a team that loved him, the respect of his competitors, and the kind of resources that most CEOs can only dream of.

But instead of staying in his sweet spot and ensuring that he and the company continued to deliver on what they did best, he made the mistake of trying to find yet another level of success. It was as if being a record holder in one sport wasn't enough; he was looking for another sport to dominate. Nick overextended and made a deal that went south. It was a big financial hit, but the company was able to absorb it. A couple of other failed ventures followed, including a product launch that had been under development for three years. Suddenly the company was reeling from not one but a series of massive losses.

I can't imagine the pressure Nick felt to outdo himself—to live up to the hype and expectations. The nonstop hours, the travel, the meetings, and the pressure almost brought him down physically too. Nick developed an ulcer, struggled with depression, and started having anxiety attacks. For a guy who was usually cool under pressure, it was very hard to see him struggling.

"I got away from what I was supposed to be doing," he told me later. "I took it too far, and it almost ruined me."

The Higher You Go

It can happen fast, much quicker than you expect. The first climbing team to ever reach the top of Everest needed more than six weeks to get up the mountain safely. What took a month and a half to conquer took only a few days to descend.

Going downhill doesn't take long. That's a bonus if you're purposely headed for base camp. But when you're trying to stay in your sweet spot at the peak, it's stunning how quickly you can lose your footing and fall.

Once you're in your dream job, people want more of you. The demands on your time and energy only increase. Expectations are higher. People are looking at you to deliver bigger results. There are also more chances for distraction once you get here—and the temptation to feed your ego becomes even greater.

After all your effort and sacrifice to get here—positioned at the intersection of your talent, passion, and mission—don't let ego, other people, or distractions pull you out of your sweet spot. The contribution you're making is too important. Keep your eye on your *why*.

Reset and Restart

The celebration of reaching your dream job marks the end of your climb to your professional pinnacle. But once the celebration ends? That's the mark of a new beginning.

Getting to the dream job means one thing: a fresh start. You're turning the page and starting a brand-new chapter. And, friends, this is where your greatest work actually begins!

To succeed in Stage 6 and guard yourself from falling like Nick, you've got to embrace that you're starting a new journey. You need to reset.

Medical students do this as they're entering their residency. They're officially doctors now—they get to wear the stethoscope with pride—but they're only just beginning. There's more work to be done, more specialized training to go through, and many, many more patients to see.

It's the same with all those athletes who get drafted into the pros each year. They've spent their entire lives working to make it big, and maybe they received a hefty signing bonus—but they start over as rookies again as a pro, working their way through the system.

What would happen if a new medical resident or a newly signed pro athlete decided to coast? They stop learning. They stop training. They just check out. Would that catapult them forward in their dream job? Of course not! That's why you've got to recognize—as you're standing at the summit—*that you've only just begun*. Now it's time to get to work.

In order for you to stay at the summit for the long haul, you'll want to be intentional about these three things:

- Set your new pace.
- Establish your reps.
- Pay attention to your inner world.

Set Your New Pace

When one of my colleagues, Riley, was in high school, she was assigned to the 400-meter race on her school track team shortly before their first meet of the season. Riley was used to running long distance. But the team was small, and the coach wanted someone in every event, so he slotted her there.

Riley had little time to figure out the nuances between running a 1,600 and a 400, and she didn't think to ask her coach. She laughs about it now, but her thought was, *Okay, this is a way shorter race. Only one lap. I can do that.* So she gunned it from the start. Around the first two turns and the far straightaway she went, feeling good. She couldn't believe it: her first 400 and she was way ahead of everybody else!

As she rounded the third turn, though, her body began resisting the pace she'd set. The muscles in her legs were on fire. Her side started aching. She got so winded that every breath was like gasping in sand. Riley slowed down in hopes of stopping the hurt. But she didn't stop, didn't give up.

Coming into the homestretch after the final turn, she still had the lead, though the other runners were closing in. It was going to be a tighter finish than she'd hoped, but she could win if she just toughed it out.

The small crowd in the stands was on its feet, cheering on the runners. Riley's eyes were on the finish line. *So close, so close! Keep going!* That's what her brain was saying, but her legs . . . they wouldn't cooperate. They were like an engine that had run out of oil. She had never hurt as badly as she was hurting right now, even after a five-mile run.

About thirty meters from the finish, past the final turn, Riley sputtered for a few steps, sucking air. It's been several years since that day, but she still remembers what happened next: "It was like a slow-motion video. I stumbled heavily, pitching forward one foot after another, almost as if I was ducking for cover. Then my legs gave way completely. I landed spread eagle on the track, embarrassed, while all the other runners passed me."

Riley didn't get back up and finish her race that day. She had nothing left in her tank to even walk the rest of the way. But she did race again, and as you'd expect, she changed her strategy for her future 400s.

The dream job will feel like the start of a 400 to you. *Ahh, this is simple—easier than what I've been doing!* You're going to be so tempted to sprint. Sometimes the excitement over your role leads to overconfidence. And sometimes you overwork to prove yourself. But we've seen the kind of damage you can do when you're trying to run too fast and push too far. Anytime you get out in front of your skis, you're going to fall.

Don't kick into some artificial pace, as if you have to go faster now and become a workaholic. Set a good pace that you can sustain by staying in the rhythms of your sweet spot.

Establish Your Reps

The second thing you want to be intentional about in order to stay at the top is to increase your reps. Let's be clear—reps are different than pace. Setting a good pace is about guarding yourself against doing *more* than your best. Upping your reps is about guarding yourself against doing *less* than your best.

Hall of Fame running back Walter Payton never quit the intensity, and he became one of the most enduring performers that professional football has ever seen. When he retired, he was the NFL's all-time leading rusher in a dozen categories. His single-game rushing record—which he set while suffering from the flu—stood for more than two decades. The nine-time Pro Bowler only missed one game in his entire thirteen-year career. Just as impressive was his consistency: ten seasons with a thousand or more yards (two of the other three were shortened by player strikes), winner of the NFL-rushing title five straight years, and an NFL Most Valuable Player title.

Opponents and teammates alike considered him a workhorse on the field. His workouts off the field were just as legendary.

In his native Mississippi, he built an obstacle-course run near the Pearl River that included sixty-five yards of sand and a levee with a steep incline. Once he moved to Chicago, he found what became known as "The Hill," a forty-five degree slope on a landfill near his home. He ran it every day during the off-season, sometimes twenty times in one session, usually during the hottest part of the day. He did this while he was becoming the NFL's number one rusher as well as when he became the league's all-time rusher. Success didn't change Payton's work ethic. Other players—elite, well-conditioned athletes themselves—would come out and try The Hill. Most of them couldn't make it to the top even once, much less back-to-back. And none of them twenty times in one day.

That conditioning was "born from pride and a desire to perform," described the *New York Times*. The way Payton put it, "If I'm going to play, I'm not going to settle for being second-best or third-best."[59]

Payton's Hill, dedicated and named in his honor in 2000, a year after his death, is now a golf course. But at the ceremony, his wife, Connie, said: "He did not run this hill to make him famous, but to become a good football player. Walter was willing to do whatever it took, and that set him apart from other players."[60]

Sometimes the harder you've had to work to get to the peak, the greater the temptation is to start coasting once you get there. All I can say is, don't fall for it. You're going to be working faster and harder in

Stage 6 than you ever have. I can't tell you how many Division 1 college football players have remarked how much quicker and tougher the NFL game is.

If you don't increase your reps now in Stage 6—if you don't continue to challenge yourself in meaningful and appropriate ways—it means you've started to coast. You've taken your foot off the gas and you're on the downhill. And brace yourself: when you start to coast, it means you've left the top.

Coasting leads to boredom. The human spirit longs for a challenge, for progress. Sir Edmund Hillary once remarked regarding a mountain: "I will come again and conquer you because as a mountain you can't grow . . . but as a human, I can."

At this stage, we make progress by challenging ourselves. Look for ways to do that for yourself. Learn something new in your field. Do something for the first time. Even taking up an extreme sport or playing an instrument reawakens the learner within us, reminding us that growth comes with challenge, and perspective comes with the new and unknown. The standouts in any field maintain their intensity, never settling for second best. They dig deeper and go harder so they can last longer—high performers to the end.

Pay Attention to Your Inner World

Third, in order to stay at the top for the long haul, you have to take care of yourself. I can't stress this enough. I think by now everybody knows the importance of good nutrition, sleep, and exercise for brain health and heart health. We hear about those things all the time. What gets fewer headlines is the need for rest and recovery. Just as your muscle groups must have rest days from working out, your heart and mind do too.

Without some margin and some downtime, mental and emotional toxins will build up. Here are a few ways you can pay attention to your inner world:

Get some quiet. You need to regularly and intentionally quiet your head and your heart. This isn't vacationing. Think personal retreats. Solo days. Morning or evening meditation. Setting aside daily, weekly, monthly, and yearly times where you can step away from the world— and from work most of all. Silence your phone, stay off of Wi-Fi, and tend to you. Just be quiet. Walk. Pray. Have some tea. Sit still. Soak in the peace. Go for a jog, not a run. Read for leisure, not for work. Journal. Let your mind relax and see what it stirs in you. This may all feel weird at first, but once you try it and learn to trust it, you'll eventually crave these regular breaks. And you'll come out of them refreshed, with a perspective and energy you didn't have beforehand.

Find a place of rest. A change of scenery does as much good as a change of schedule. Where can you be quiet and turn down the white noise of busyness? It doesn't have to cost you a dime. It could be as simple as spending an afternoon sitting under a shade tree in your backyard or on your balcony, finding a quiet corner at a library or a remote bench at a park. Or you can go hiking or fishing in the great outdoors. For some people, a day at a museum or a classical concert lets them chill. You probably know what works for you and what doesn't. If you don't know yet, experiment. Your inner self will thank you.

Make yourself accountable. We were made for connection. You cannot keep yourself upright (and at the top!) without other people.

Find at least one accountability partner. Not your spouse or anyone who's related to you. Find someone who is objective, who will challenge your thinking, and most of all, who feels no obligation whatsoever to agree with you! Because as soon as you've surrounded yourself with yes people, you're headed for trouble.

If you don't have this voice of reason in your life already, seek someone out. Choose wisely because you're going to be hanging all your laundry out to dry in front of them. I've relied on close friends, colleagues, and mentors to make sure that my head and heart are healthy and focused on the right things.

Some people prefer group accountability; others like a one-on-one thing, where they're sitting down with a mentor, a life coach, a pastor, or a counselor. Either way works. But to stay on top, make this a regular practice.

Stay the Course

For three decades, other climbers had attempted to reach the top of Everest, only to be defeated by the mountain, the weather, inadequate resources, or poor strategies. The British team that New Zealander Edmund Hillary and his Nepal guide, Tenzing Norgay, were part of in 1953 was the ninth hopeful expedition.

Just three days before Hillary and Norgay's attempt at the summit, another team from their group had tried but turned back some three hundred feet short of the goal. The extra-long climb and difficult conditions on that day left those men without the energy and oxygen reserves to complete the last leg and safely reach camp afterwards. They couldn't stay the course to finish the dream.

Hillary and Norgay camped significantly higher the night before their attempt, which enabled them to reach the pinnacle in five hours, with enough left over to make it back to their companions before dark.

Whether it's just before the peak or once you've reached it, don't cut your trip short. How does it happen at this stage? One word: *burnout.*

In addition to paying attention to your pace, your reps, and your inner world, in Stage 6, you need to guard against burnout. Gallup did a study of almost 7,500 full-time employees and found that about two-thirds of them have experienced burnout on the job.[61] You may know the feeling all too well. You don't want to get out of bed and face another day at the job. You're emotionally spent and physically exhausted. Your drive to work is a battle to distract yourself from your desperation. You've lost your enthusiasm for the work, and every spark of excitement you once had for the results you produce is gone. It's your dream job, but you're miserable.

Burnout happens when stress and exhaustion from your job build up so much that it drains your energy and robs you of your sense of purpose. And it affects every part of your life—your work, your relationships, and your health.

The Five Causes of Burnout

As I talk to people about their problems with burnout, I've come to realize that burnout is the symptom, not the cause of their misery.

The cause is buildup on the heart, and there are five main reasons for it:

1. **I've lost my passion for the work.** The work that once gave you the juice and the results you were once so proud of have lost their shine. You've lost the feeling of fulfillment. When your job stops mattering so much, you begin to believe that your work doesn't matter either. Then, you start believing that *you* don't matter. It's a spiral that can quickly lead to buildup.

2. **My workplace is toxic.** Poor leadership, gossipy coworkers, or teammates who don't trust one another is downright draining. No matter how hard you try to have a good attitude, that kind of negativity day after day will crush your spirit.

3. **I'm bored to death.** You can love your line of work but hit a wall because you're doing the same tasks day in and day out. When you don't feel challenged or aren't making something that's meaningful to you, your motivation will grow slim. This can also happen when you're overqualified for the job you have and running on autopilot.

4. **I feel completely overwhelmed.** You feel like you're drowning as soon as you pull into the parking lot. Your workload is too much for one person. Staying late each night and wrecking your personal life are enough to make anyone's motivation go downhill. You know you're drowning when it's so bad that you can't relax and have fun—and even though you fall into bed exhausted, you can't sleep.

5. **I feel underappreciated**. Everyone needs to feel appreciated. That doesn't mean you need constant awards, applause, and pats on the back. But if you've gone months or years without having your hard work recognized, that starts to hurt.

Folks, the feelings of exhaustion and hopelessness you're experiencing are very real. But let me encourage you: you're not *really* burned out. The only time you truly "burn out" is the day you die. That means you have time to turn your situation around. If you're reading this early enough, you can even do a little preventative maintenance.

Let's call those feelings what they are: *buildup*. A buildup of too much negativity from your workplace. Like plaque on your teeth, it can be so gradual that you don't even notice it. Then one day, you look in the mirror and realize you've got a problem.

Take a moment and put your hand on your heart. You can feel your heartbeat, right? But if you added more and more layers of clothing, eventually you would no longer feel your heartbeat. You'd be breathing, so you'd know your heart is beating in there somewhere, but you can't feel it.

With buildup, you're in your dream job, but you don't feel alive anymore. You can't feel your heart beating.

Resolving Buildup

What you need to know is that buildup isn't the end of your journey. *It can actually be a new beginning for you*. Always remember: you were designed to play a unique role in life. Someone out there needs you to be you—so don't let buildup stand in the way of doing what you were made to do! You *can* get back to feeling excited to go to work each day.

If you're truly drained, recovery may take a while—a weekend getaway or a good night's sleep won't fix it. You may even need more than one approach. Here are a few ways to get back on track:

***Rediscover your* why.** No matter what else you do, be sure you do this. Go back to the purpose statement you wrote earlier in chapter 2. Why was this your dream job in the first place? What drew you? Has anything changed? Have you changed? Evaluate:

- Do I still genuinely enjoy the work I do right now?
- Do I still connect with the results my work produces?
- Am I tapping into what I do best (my talent) and what I love to do most (my passion)?

You may be tired of hearing me say it, but your sweet spot has to go with you—even when you're at the top. No matter how high you go, you'll be the happiest and most fulfilled when you're in your sweet spot. I wish my friend Nick could have recognized the value he added just by bringing his best self to his work. He had enough going on as a CEO in his sweet spot. Thankfully, he realizes this now.

Some of your advisors may push you to create more wows, more headlines. You may believe that's what's next. But your dream job isn't an up-the-ante situation, where you have to leave your sweet spot to explore an unproven place. You don't need to live up to anything except the best of who you are and what you can do.

Locate the source. Another way to dissolve buildup is to ask, *Where's the source? Who or what is contaminating the waters?*

If you're in a toxic environment, is it the culture itself? Or more specifically, is it a teammate? Your leader? A 2020 Achievers report showed that only 23 percent of employees in 2020 felt that senior leadership was very or highly engaged in improving company culture.[62] That means three in four employees are being led by people who seem lackluster or completely ambivalent about creating a great workplace.

Locating the source will help you determine the course of action and how drastic or simple it needs to be. See what it will take to eliminate that source of buildup. It may take less than you think for your passion to return.

Speak up. I always recommend talking with your leader before making any major changes. If you have way too much on your plate, ask him or her to help you prioritize and set boundaries. If people around you are gossiping or stabbing each other in the back, bring it to your leader first and *then*—if appropriate—talk with your coworkers directly. Communication is key to a healthy work environment. If your leader isn't willing to truly lead in these areas by helping you reach a solution, then you may have good reason to start looking for a new job.

Change your perspective. This one's not always easy, but sometimes you need to adjust *your* attitude and see your job in a new light. Instead of focusing on the fact that you're dissatisfied, put your Reticular Activating System to work and focus on the good things. What is your job helping you accomplish right now? What about it are you thankful for? As you do this, you'll begin to see it in a different light— and look forward to what's coming in the future.

Feeling underappreciated is a particularly difficult concern that needs perspective. Nearly every employee study reports that a lack of recognition—whether in pay raises, praise, or promotion—is the main reason people leave their jobs. Try to take a step back and look objectively to see if you really are being overlooked or if it's more of a reflection of the buildup you're feeling.

Do you require more affirmation or reward than your coworkers? Are others being recognized and you're not? Or are you in a place where no one is recognized? If it's a feeling, then admit it, talk it out with someone you can trust, and change your perspective. If it's a fact, then plan to have a conversation with your leader. You might just be a catalyst for change for yourself and your coworkers.

Change your role. Maybe you love the company you work for, but there's a different role that would better suit your unique skills and passions. With any open internal positions that interest and fit you, you first want to run it through each aspect of your purpose statement to stay in your sweet spot. Then talk with your leader about the possibility of making a switch *before* you make any inquiries. You don't want your interest in a different position to get back to your leader from a third party.

Change your location. Dave Ramsey says your dream job is like your dream house—once you get it, at some point it stops being your dream house. The kids grow up, move out, and then the dream looks different. The house no longer fits, and you decide to make a change.

That's okay. Nothing is permanent. One year the job may absolutely be what you're looking for, but as people come and go and the company evolves over time, things change. *You* become a different person too. What you're looking for may change over time. You're not required to stay in this job for the rest of your life. Just be very cautious not to jump ship too quickly. You want to run *to* something, not *away* from something.

The Finish Line

When people think about Stages 6 and 7 on the path to meaningful work, they envision the finish line, the end of a great climb. And while that certainly makes sense, it's more like a surprise ending because the end is really just a new beginning. There's still so much ahead—and it's bigger and better than what you can imagine right now.

Another surprise you may not be expecting is that Stages 6 and 7 happen at the same time. Instead of being linear like the other stages, these two go hand in hand. So soak in the goodness, accomplishment, and focus of today, but know that the best is yet to come.

Your best is yet to come.

Chapter 12 Takeaways

Remember This

Don't forget why you are here and what got you here.

You Got This

Stay grounded and you will stay on top.

Do This

Review the five causes of burnout and examine your work life.

STAGE 7

Give Yourself Away to Work Like No One Else

13

Expand Your Vision

G rowing up, he had said he wanted to see the world. And now he was.

Explorer Edmund Hillary had just summited Mount Everest with his climbing partner, Sherpa Tenzing Norgay. It was shortly before noon on the morning of May 29, 1953. The two men were standing at airplane altitude, five and a half miles in the sky, with the entire world below them. At the pinnacle of planet Earth (and their careers as climbers), these rugged adventurers shook hands—all civilized—and then Norgay, unable to contain the thrill of the moment, wrapped Hillary up in a huge bear hug.

After taking some pictures and leaving some mementos at the peak, each man spent a few minutes taking it all in. Scanning the world from above 29,000 feet, Hillary found himself gazing across a valley toward another towering peak, Makalu, and working out a route in his mind for how it could be climbed. He said of that moment, "It showed me that even though I was standing on top of the world, it wasn't the end of everything. I was still looking beyond to other interesting challenges."[63]

Can you imagine it? Hillary's body is exhausted after the dangerous five-hour climb to the summit amid bitter winds and drifting snows. Yet he is re-energized by a view, a visual, he's never had before. In every sense of the word he has *realized* this dream of conquering the world's highest peak—he has *made real* something he had only envisioned until now. And what does he do next, while literally standing on top of the world? He dreams another dream!

It reminds me of something that was said about Ferdinand Magellan's sail around the globe: "The real significance of Magellan's voyage was not that it was the first to circumnavigate the planet, but that it was the first to realize just how big that planet was."[64]

This is what it's about! Right there. Both Hillary and Magellan accomplished massive dreams—going where no one had gone before—and then they saw: there's even more out there.

At the Top

Until now, you've been looking *up* at this mountain and striving for the goal. But once you get to the top, you're looking *out*, not up. You can see so much more, and you realize, *Ahh, it's even bigger than I imagined!*

That's the beauty of this final stage of the journey. *As our vision expands, so do our dreams.*

I think this caught Edmund Hillary by surprise. I mean, I wouldn't expect to start plotting my sequel *at the same moment* I realized such an enormous dream, would you? And yet the view from the top is the clearest. So it's really the perfect birthplace for another dream.

I love this idea that one dream births another. From the top of this mountain, you catch sight of the next one. And you take all that you learned from this journey to succeed in that future adventure. We see this in Hillary's conquests after Everest. He not only summited ten other Himalayan peaks, but he also reached both the South and the North Poles in his lifetime.

But there was a deeply personal result of Hillary's experience that we don't dare miss either: *as his vision grew, so did his heart for others.*

Through his ascent of Everest, Hillary developed an enduring friendship with Norgay. "I have never regarded myself as a hero," said Hillary at a tribute ceremony in Darjeeling several years after Norgay's death. "But Tenzing undoubtedly was."

Inspired by this friendship and the needs he saw within the Sherpa community, Hillary devoted himself to helping these unsung heroes of Everest—"my dear friends in the Himalaya," as he called them—through the Himalayan Trust, a nonprofit he established in 1960 and oversaw until his death almost fifty years later.

As the first man in human history to have ever stood at both the North and South Poles *and* summit Everest, you'd think he would have considered his outdoor conquests his greatest achievements. His accomplishments earned him headlines around the world and inspired legions of other explorers. But when asked about the results he was most proud of, he often spoke of his humanitarian work: "Of all the things I have done, exciting though many of them have been, there's no doubt in my mind that the most worthwhile have been the establishing of schools and hospitals, and the rebuilding of monasteries in the mountains."[65, 66]

Throughout his career, he did *what* he loved—exploring—until his body couldn't do it anymore. And he saw unprecedented success. But it was discovering *who* he loved—a people he loved—that led to his greatest work, his greatest mission, of all.

So while Everest was the birthplace of his future adventures, it also opened his eyes and his heart to a community of people in need that he would never have known otherwise. A community he would invest in until the day he died. A community that will be reaping the effects of his love and generosity for generations to come.

Give Yourself Away

How your vision and heart expand in Stage 7 turns the tables completely. You discover what changes inside of us on this journey is even more important than all that happens to us.

At the top of the mountain, you see more clearly than ever where the needs are. You see who you can help that you'd never known about until now. You see how you can help—and you're able to help in ways that you couldn't before. You realize the dreams others have, and you want *their* dreams to come true just like yours have.

Now you're in a position to give yourself away like never before.

Bruce still vividly remembers what it was like to have only two shirts and two pairs of pants as a kid growing up in an alcoholic home. Because of his upbringing, the sight of poverty has always made him sad, and he decided long ago to do something about it.

He saw so much of it while serving in the US Army in Vietnam that it broke his heart. That breaking of his heart gave him a purpose that has never gone away.

After he and three of his Army buddies returned from Vietnam, they started a co-op that—three generations later—is still changing lives. The organization employs 120 agricultural workers, almost all of whom have families. Bruce has contributed over a quarter of a million dollars so far to the project, and he returns regularly to Vietnam to invest in the lives of those families. To him, he's completing not a career mission but his life's mission.

I'll be honest, this isn't the easiest stage for me to talk about because I've barely begun it myself. I reached my dream job in September 2017, but I'm only now really beginning to expand the dream. Right now, I'm watching what the other dreamers ahead of me are doing. I'm taking note of the ways they give themselves away. People like Bruce who regularly invest in other people and quietly give away large sums of money.

Like Judy Faulkner, America's wealthiest self-made woman in tech who regularly donates to local charities each year and has pledged to donate at least half of her $2.5 billion fortune.

Like Sara Blakely, the founder and owner of Spanx, whose foundation helps educate and empower women.

What they're doing is what I want for you and me. These people aren't just realizing their ever-expanding dreams. They're fulfilling the promise of their potential and using all the good they've gained to change as many lives as they can, for as long as they can.

What They Need

I first learned of this idea of giving yourself away just before I went to college. It was included in a book of quotes that the teachers at our high school had given each graduating senior. As I was packing up for my first semester away from home, I stopped and flipped through the pages, landing on a quote by business guru Zig Ziglar: "Help people get what they want and you'll always have what you need."

What a lightning bolt that was! I couldn't believe how much sense that made!

As a young adult, about to leave home for the first time, these were words I could take with me to help me stand out and make friends. They also seemed straight out of the career-politician's playbook, back when I was expecting politics to be my career path. In my teenaged ambition, this made sense as a path to *my* goals: *Okay, I need to help as many people win so I can win. I'll do that if it means I get what I want!*

So from my first week on campus, I went around offering to help anybody with anything. I volunteered to help with student events, student government, and even local political campaigns in my college town. And sure enough, it was almost impossible for people to turn me down! I made lots of friends that year. And just as Ziglar said, I got what I wanted: I made a bit of a name for myself as a freshman.

Only I had Ziglar's words turned inside out. My focus was me. The heart behind it was for me. I wasn't helping for their sake. Not really. It was fun, but it's like I had the dreamer's telescope turned backwards.

Loving your work and doing what you were born to do produces a greater passion: doing more of what you love for more of the people you grow to love. *Your standard becomes love.* Loving what you do and why. Loving the results you create. Loving the people you get to impact. There's no higher motive, no higher cause.

The great composer Mozart said, "Neither a lofty degree of intelligence nor imagination nor both together go to the making of genius. Love, love, love, that is the soul of genius."

At age seventeen, I read Ziglar's quote and believed the words because of what I could *get*. It wasn't until I became a husband and a father that I understood it as a call to how much I can *give*.

Someday you and I will retire. One day we will die. And no matter how great our status, a generation will eventually be born that won't recognize our names. But the results we produce through our dream work and the people we impact thanks to the love within us—these will outlast us. Giving ourselves away in love is our life's work.

For the Love

Not long ago, I caught a conversation between two cultural icons. Jerry Seinfeld was being interviewed by Howard Stern, and they were discussing what it takes to be great at what you do. Stern recalled his journey to radio and all the work it involved, and said, "It is possible to will yourself . . . [to] get what you want."

Seinfeld interjected:

What you were using, what Michael Jordan uses, and what I use, it's not will. It's love. When you love something, it's a bottomless pool of energy. . . . But you have to love it, sincerely. Not because you're going to make money from it or be famous or get whatever you want to get. When you do it because you love it, then you can find yourself moving up and getting really good at something. . . .

Will is like not eating dessert or something; that's just forcing yourself. You can't force yourself to do, to be what you have made yourself into. You can love it. Love is endless. Will is finite. . . .

Real love is what enables you to accomplish anything. Not discipline, not work ethic. You gotta love it. If you love it, those other things come in behind it. They're the troops behind. Love is the general.[67]

There is no greater conquest or higher summit in your work or your life than to give yourself away.

As you travel Stages 6 and 7 on your path to meaningful work, you will soon realize the path is actually a circle. As your vision and heart expand, you'll soon find yourself back at Stage 1 to Get Clear, and continue circling the stages for the rest of your career.

Where will love take you?

Where will your dream lead you next?

The pen of your legacy is in your hand.

Who are the people you want to help?

What are the problems you want to solve?

What are the solutions you want to provide?

The world needs what you have to offer and is waiting for you to do what you were born to do.

Remember This

As our vision expands, so do our dreams.

You Got This

Your heart led you here. Let it lead you forward.

Do This

Never stop giving yourself away!

CONCLUSION

.

"Duty is ours. Results are God's."

— JOHN QUINCY ADAMS

During my basketball-playing days, the most valuable lesson I ever learned—the lesson I've taken with me—is something my dad would tell me before each game:

Leave it all on the floor.

To the best of my ability, I took his advice and gave it all I had. Every game.

Until the final buzzer sounded.

I love that these were always Dad's parting words to me. He was talking about heart. He was urging me, challenging me, to listen to my heart and create results that would make my heart sing.

He also knew that if I played my guts out, leaving nothing in the tank, my team might win. Then the victory would feel even sweeter for my effort. But no matter the final score, or even if I didn't play so well on a particular night, I would know that I gave everything I had, and so would my team.

This is what I want you to hear as you exit our "locker room" and head out onto the court: leave it all on the floor.

Every industry, every job field, every company is looking for people who know their unique role, who love what they do, and who will show up every day and give it their all with a fierce sense of purpose. I've set you up to do just that.

As your coach over the past thirteen chapters, I've given you the entire path to the win. I've laid out the process for clarity, told you what to expect, how to overcome the obstacles and emotions you'll face, and which questions to ask of yourself and others. It's all here and it *will* change your life . . . but only if you get out there and get after it.

The choice is yours. You have everything you need. But only you can choose to step out. Only you can choose to stay focused and keep showing up, day after day and year after year. No one else can do it for you.

It's time for you to hit the floor and offer up your best for a world, a workplace, and a whole lot of people who need you. Nobody else can do it your way, with your heart, your vision, and your gifts. And someday, when the clock hits 0:00 on the final game at the end of your career, you'll be able to reminisce and not regret.

You'll reminisce on where you started—and where you finished.

On how hard it was—and how rewarding it was.

On how scary it was—and how exciting.

You'll reminisce about the problems you solved—and the people who were directly helped by your solutions.

Looking back, you'll know the exhilaration of a race run well. Best of all, your heart will be overflowing. You gave yourself away! Gave everything you had! Heart and soul. Passion and purpose.

For the love of it.

Give your dream all you've got. Get out there and be the very best version of you. It won't be perfect—and it doesn't have to be. But do all you can to be all you can to make the greatest impact you can.

Put down the book and start. Start now, and don't quit.

The ball is in your hands. Your team and I and all your fans are counting on you to run the floor and do what you were born for. All in. Everything you got. Till the buzzer sounds. No excuses, no regrets.

Do you hear me? I'm talking to you and you alone in this moment.

YOU were created to fill a unique role.

YOU are needed.

YOU matter deeply.

YOU have what it takes to make a difference in this world.

YOU must do it.

Don't overthink it. Just follow the plan we've worked on. Take what we've talked about, what we've practiced, and then do as my dad said: leave it all on the floor.

Somebody out there needs you. Follow your heart, and press on!

NOTES

1. "2020 Engagement and Retention Report: Failure to Engage," Achievers (October 7, 2019). https://www.achievers.com/wp-content/uploads/2020/10/012220_Achievers_ERR_124-1.pdf.

2. U.S. Bureau of Labor Statistics, "Number of Jobs, Labor Market Experience, and Earnings Growth: Results From a National Longitudinal Survey," (August 22, 2019). https://www.bls.gov/news.release/pdf/nlsoy.pdf.

3. Jennifer Liu, "Career Change Report: An Inside Look at Why Workers Shift Gears," Indeed (October 30, 2019). https://www.indeed.com/lead/career-change.

4. Shawn Achor, Andrew Reece, Gabriella Rosen Kellerman, and Alexi Robichaux, "9 Out of 10 People Are Willing to Earn Less Money to Do More-Meaningful Work," *Harvard Business Review* (November 6, 2018). https://hbr.org/2018/11/9-out-of-10-people-are-willing-to-earn-less-money-to-do-more-meaningful-work.

5. *Lexico*, s.v. "clarity," accessed August 8, 2021, https://www.lexico.com/en/definition/clarity.

6. Kendra Cherry, "The Psychology of Flow," Verywell Mind (January 13, 2021). https://www.verywellmind.com/what-is-flow-2794768.

7. Mihaly Csikszentmihalyi, "Flow, the Secret to Happiness," filmed at an official TED conference (February 2004), video, 18:43. https://www.ted.com/talks/mihaly_csikszentmihalyi_flow_the_secret_to_happiness/up-next?language=en.

8. Mary Fecteau, "Martin Luther King Jr.'s Powerful Message to Cleveland Students," *Ideastream* (January 20, 2019). https://www.ideastream.org/news/martin-luther-king-jr-s-powerful-message-to-cleveland-students.

9. Michael Tomaszewski, "Hard Skills: Definition & List of Best Examples for Any Resume," Zety (February 5, 2021). https://zety.com/blog/hard-skills.

10. Ken Coleman, *One Question* (New York: Howard Books, 2013), 36–37.

11. Coleman, 35–36.

12. Federal Reserve Bank of New York, "The Labor Market for Recent College Graduates: Underemployment Rates for College Graduates," (February 12, 2021). https://www.newyorkfed.org/research/college-labor-market/college-labor-market_underemployment_rates.html.

13. National Center for Educational Statistics, *Employment and Unemployment Rates by Educational Attainment*, Institute of Education Sciences, May 2021, https://nces.ed.gov/programs/coe/indicator/cbc.

14. U.S. Bureau of Labor Statistics, "Multiple Jobholders as a Percent of Employed [LNU02026620]," FRED, Federal Reserve Bank of St. Louis (February 23, 2021). https://fred.stlouisfed.org/series/LNU02026620.

15. Glenn Kessler, "Harris on People Working Multiple Jobs," *The Washington Post* (June 27, 2019). https://www.washingtonpost.com/politics/2019/live-updates/general-election/fact-checking-the-first-democratic-debate/harris-on-people-working-multiple-jobs/?arc404=true.

16. *Sports Illustrated* staff, "How Serena Williams Gets in Her Opponent's Head and Mounts a Comeback," *Sports Illustrated* (May 12, 2015) MasterClass video, 1:56, https://www.si.com/tennis/video/2015/05/12/serena-williams-art-of-comeback.

17. Denise Stromme and Lori Rothstein, "Episode 1.5," *Two for You*, University of Minnesota Extension, (October 10, 2017) video, 2:18, https://extension.umn.edu/two-you-video-series/ras.

18. Sharon Linde, "Introduction to Psychology: Reticular Activating System: Definition & Function," Study.com (August 23, 2016) video, 5:20, https://study.com/academy/lesson/reticular-activating-system-definition-function.html.

19. Tobias van Schneider, "If You Want It, You Might Get It. The Reticular Activating System Explained," Desk of van Schneider, Medium (June 22, 2017). https://medium.com/desk-of-van-schneider/if-you-want-it-you-might-get-it-the-reticular-activating-system-explained-761b6ac14e53

20. BeckmanInstitute, "The Invisible Gorilla (Featuring Daniel Simons)—EMMY Winner," February 14, 2011, YouTube video, 4:45, https://www.youtube.com/watch?v=UtKt8YF7dgQ&pbjreload=101.

21. The Albert Team, "Positive and Negative Feedback Loops in Biology," Albert (June 1, 2020). https://www.albert.io/blog/positive-negative-feedback-loops-biology/.

22. Ashley Mateo, "How to Run a Marathon with the 10/10/10 Method," *Runner's World* (October 4, 2019). https://www.runnersworld.com/training/a29342955/marathon-training-strategy/.

23. Robert Eisele, "Chosen for the Team," *The Great Debaters*, directed by Denzel Washington (Chicago: Harpo Films, 2007) Movieclips video, 1:58, https://www.youtube.com/watch?v=k95b72QHu60.

24. Mark S. Granovetter, "The Strength of Weak Ties," *American Journal of Sociology*, Vol. 78, Issue 6 (May 1973), 1371. https://sociology.stanford.edu/sites/g/files/sbiybj9501/f/publications/the_strength_of_weak_ties_and_exch_w-gans.pdf.

25. Granovetter, 1372.

26. Vivian Giang, "What LinkedIn Data Reveals About Who Will Help You Get Your Next Job," *Fast Company* blog (June 14, 2016). https://www.fastcompany.com/3060887/what-linkedin-data-reveals-about-who-will-help-you-get-your-next-job.

27. Granovetter, "The Strength of Weak Ties," 1371.

28. Scott Swedberg, "Is Landing a Job Really About Who You Know?" The Job Sauce blog (July 1, 2020). https://thejobsauce.com/is-landing-a-job-really-about-who-you-know/.

29. Scott Swedberg, "The Two Worst Ways to Search for a Job (And One Way That Works)," *Forbes* blog (February 12, 2020). https://www.forbes.com/sites/forbescoachescouncil/2020/02/12/the-two-worst-ways-to-search-for-a-job-and-one-way-that-works/#1f6801f7f60e.

30. 2 Corinthians 9:6–7 (ESV).

31. Glenn Guilbeau, "Ex-Cajuns AD Saw 'It' in DabO, So Could O Have It, Too?" *USA Today Network* (January 15, 2017). https://www.theadvertiser.com/story/sports/college /lsu/2017/01/14/ex-cajuns-ad-saw-dabo-could-o-have-too/96545068/.

32. Chris Low, "Meet the Man Who Always Believed in Dabo Swinney," *ESPN*, (January 9, 2017). https://www.espn.com/college-football/story/_/id/18441434/clemson -tigers-dabo-swinney-national-champion-thanks-man-hired-believed-him.

33. Swedberg, "Is Landing a Job Really About Who You Know?"

34. Swedberg, "Is Landing a Job Really About Who You Know?"

35. Ken Coleman, "Why You Should Network Like Introverts," *Ladders* (June 6, 2019). https://www.theladders.com/career-advice/why-you-should-network-like-introverts.

36. Dr. Tony Evans, "Feelings and Truth," *The Urban Alternative*. https://tonyevans .org/feelings-and-truth/.

37. Dr. Alice Boyes, "How to Overcome Your Fear of Making Mistakes," *Harvard Business Review*, (June 24, 2020). https://hbr.org/2020/06/how-to-overcome-your -fear-of-making-mistakes.

38. Patrick Henry, "Give Me Liberty Or Give Me Death," (speech, Richmond, VA, March 23, 1775), University of Minnesota Human Rights Library. http://hrlibrary.umn.edu /education/libertyordeath.html.

39. Alan Arnette, "Everest by the Numbers: 2019 Edition," *The Blog on alanarnette.com* (December 17, 2017). https://www.alanarnette.com/blog/2017/12/17 /everest-by-the-numbers-2018-edition/.

40. Shannon Ables, "The Difference Between Being Scared and Having Doubts," *The Simply Luxurious Life*, January 28, 2019, emphasis added, https://thesimplyluxuriouslife .com/the-difference-between-being-scared/.

41. Ables, "The Difference Between Being Scared and Having Doubts."

42. Zechariah 4:10 (paraphrased from English Standard Version and New Living Translation).

43. Matthew 14:22–33.

44. Ken Coleman, *One Question*, 74–75.

45. Dr. Noam Shpancer, "Designed for Success," *Psychology Today* (October 7, 2020). https://www.psychologytoday.com/us/articles/202008/designed-success.

46. Cathy Free, "This School Janitor Has Quietly Been Giving Homeless Students Clothes, Soap and More From Her 'Giving Closet,'" *The Washington Post* (September 4, 2018). https://www.washingtonpost.com/news/inspired-life/wp/2018/09/04/this-school -janitor-has-been-quietly-been-giving-homeless-students-clothes-soap-and-more-from-her -care-closet/.

47. John C. Maxwell, *The 15 Invaluable Laws of Growth* (Nashville, TN: Center Street, 2012), 20.

48. Tim Sanders, *The Likeability Factor* (New York: Three Rivers Press, 2006), 211.

49. Tim Sanders, "The Likeability Factor," timsanders.com (May 24, 2019). https:// timsanders.com/books/likeability-factor/.

50. Sanders, *The Likeability Factor*, 18.

51. Pat Summitt with Sally Jenkins, *Sum It Up* (New York: Crown Archetype, 2013), 214–215, emphasis added.

52. Hebrews 12:11 (CEV).

53. Pat Summitt with Sally Jenkins, *Sum It Up* (New York: Three Rivers Press, 2014), 240.

54. Brené Brown, *Rising Strong* (New York: Random House, 2015), 4.

55. Daniel Kahneman and Angus Deaton, "High Income Improves Evaluation of Life but Not Emotional Well-Being," Center for Health and Wellbeing, Princeton University (August 4, 2010). https://www.princeton.edu/~deaton/downloads/deaton_kahneman_high_income_improves_evaluation_August2010.pdf.

56. NEA Research, "Rankings of the States 2019 and Estimates of School Statistics 2020," National Education Association (June 2020). https://www.nea.org/sites/default/files/2020-07/2020%20Rankings%20and%20Estimates%20Report%20FINAL_0.pdf.

57. Sylvia Allegretto and Lawrence Mishel, "Teacher Pay Penalty Dips but Persists in 2019," Economic Policy Institute (September 17, 2020). https://www.epi.org/publication/teacher-pay-penalty-dips-but-persists-in-2019-public-school-teachers-earn-about-20-less-in-weekly-wages-than-nonteacher-college-graduates/.

58. Robert D. McFadden, "Edmund Hillary, First on Everest, Dies at 88," *The New York Times* (January 10, 2008). https://www.nytimes.com/2008/01/10/world/asia/11cnd-hillary.html.

59. Ira Berkow, "For Two, a Long Wait Ends at the Top; Walter Payton," *The New York Times* (January 26, 1986). https://www.nytimes.com/1986/01/26/sports/for-two-a-long-wait-ends-at-the-top-walter-payton.html.

60. Lisa Black, "Payton's Hill Dedicated," *Chicago Tribune* (May 14, 2000). https://www.chicagotribune.com/news/ct-xpm-2000-05-14-0005140178-story.html.

61. Ben Wigert and Sangeeta Agrawal, "Employee Burnout, Part 1: The 5 Main Causes," Gallup (July 12, 2018). https://www.gallup.com/workplace/237059/employee-burnout-part-main-causes.aspx.

62. Achievers, *Engagement & Retention*.

63. "The Adventure to the Top of the World," Primus (n.d.). https://primus.us/pages/the-adventure-to-the-top-of-the-world.

64. Bill Bryson, *At Home*, (Toronto: Doubleday Canada, 2010), 175.

65. Hazel Plush, "'Life's Like Mountaineering—Never Look Down': The Wisdom of Sir Edmund Hillary," *The Telegraph* (July 20, 2016). https://www.telegraph.co.uk/travel/destinations/asia/nepal/articles/quotes-sir-edmund-hillary-first-man-climb-everest/.

66. https://www.quotetab.com/quote/by-edmund-hillary.

67. Howard Stern, "Video: Jerry Seinfeld on Whether '23 Hours to Kill' Is His Final Stand-Up Special and Which Other Comedian Could've Played Cosmo Kramer," *The Howard Stern Show*, SiriusXM (May 20, 2020). https://www.howardstern.com/show/2020/05/20/video-jerry-seinfeld-whether-23-hours-kill-his-final-stand-special-and-which-other-comedian-couldve-played-cosmo-kramer/.

Discover your purpose with America's Career Coach.

To have your career questions answered, check out
The Ken Coleman Show on your favorite platform.